Peter Haining is the author of the definitive biography of *Sweeney Todd: The Real Story of the Demon Barber of Fleet Street* (1993) – the serial killer who dispatched more than a hundred and sixty victims and then had his female accomplice turn their flesh into meat pies. He has also written about a number of other famous crimes and criminals and edited a series of best-selling anthologies including *Murder on the Menu* (1991) and *Murder by the Glass* (1994), both intended for readers with strong stomachs. He lives in Suffolk.

Cannibal Killers

Peter Haining

Magpie Books, London

Constable & Robinson Ltd
3 The Lanchesters
162 Fulham Palace Road
London W6 9ER
www.constablerobinson.com

This edition published by Magpie Books,
an imprint of Constable & Robinson Ltd 2005

First published in the UK by Boxtree, 1994

A copy of the British Library Cataloguing in
Publication Data is available from the British Library

ISBN 1-84529-178-6
ISBN 978-1-84529-178-5

Printed and bound in the EU

3 5 7 9 10 8 6 4 2

Contents

CANNIBALISM. Man-eating, also known as anthropophagy; the eating of the human body or parts of it, or the drinking of human blood, by human beings. The emotions which cannibalism arouses are powerful.

Funk & Wagnalls Dictionary of Folklore, Mythology and Legend (1975)

Introduction: When Man Eats Man

In the summer of 1986, an international team of scientists excavating a Stone Age dwelling inside the Fontbregoua Cave in the hills of Provence in south-eastern France made an astonishing discovery. In what they had at first imagined to be just a shallow refuse pit used by the cave dwellers some 6,000 years ago, the anthropologists found a number of bones which they now believe to be the earliest – and most convincing – evidence of the practice of cannibalism by humans.

As the team carefully sifted through the refuse in the pit, they uncovered the butchered remains of six people – three adults, two children and one of indeterminate age – which had lain undisturbed there for six millennia. The excavators also found several other deposits of human bones in the cave, but there was clear evidence that all of these had been disturbed by animals at some point in time.

Immediately following the discovery in the pit,

the bones of the six were analysed under an electron microscope. This revealed that all had been stripped of their flesh with stone axes very shortly after death had occurred. The arm and leg bones had also been cracked in order to gain access to the nutritious marrow inside; and there were signs, too, that they had probably been cooked over a fire before being eaten.

The leader of the research team, Dr Paola Villa from the University of Colorado, announced the discovery in the journal *Science* on 18 July 1986. He stated quite unequivocally, 'I am convinced that this is the first true instance of cannibalism that has been proved.'

What Dr Villa and his team believed to be so important about this find was the fact that the bones had not been moved or gnawed by animals during the thousands of years they had laid hidden in the cave. For often in the past when ancient bones giving the impression of being butchered had been turned up by scientists, further investigation had proved that they had actually been scavenged by animals or else used in burial rituals which involved the cutting up of the remains.

Popular mythology has, of course, for many years propounded a world of bestial Neanderthals and flesh-eating jungle tribes. Some anthropologists, however, have disputed the fact that cannibalism has *ever* been systematically practised by human beings. Although, they admit, there are many reports about primitive groups who apparently ate one another, eyewitness accounts of such acts taking place are very rare. Consequently, the case for and against the existence of the practice has raged among the academics for years.

There are, for instance, those scientists who accept that the ancient Aztecs practised cannibalism because it gave them important nutritional advantages; while on the other hand some authorities have equally strongly disputed accounts that the tribesmen in New Guinea regarded eating human flesh as ethically and socially acceptable.

Whatever these debaters may say, however, the history books undoubtedly contain a large number of accounts of people eating one another: stories which date from earliest times to the present day and range in their locations across much of the world. In literature, too, the evidence of fascination with the subject is readily found. Shakespeare, for one, wrote in *Othello*:

'It was my hint to speak, such was the process
And of the Cannibals that each other eat.'

Likewise, the eighteenth-century man of letters Jonathan Swift could not resist satirising the subject in an attack on the politicians and landlords who oppressed and starved the poor – demonstrating as he did so that the topic was as familiar in his day as it had already been for many centuries:

'I have been assured,' he wrote in 1728, 'by a very knowing American of my acquaintance in London, that a young healthy child well nursed is, at a year old, a most delicious, nourishing and wholesome food, whether stewed, roasted, baked or boiled; and I make no doubt that it will equally well serve in a fricassee or a ragout.'

Just recently we have had that intrepid explorer Colonel John Blashford-Snell expounding his belief that Colonel H P Fawcett who disappeared in the Amazon jungle in 1925 was eaten by cannibals. And if support was needed for the view that the practice continues in that part of South America, this emerged only a couple of years ago in the form of a documentary movie shown in Italy and Spain, *Cannibal Holocaust*, which featured the gruesome tale of four journalists captured and eaten by the fearsome Shatamari cannibals living in a remote area of the Orinoco basin.

This book, however, is not intended either as an argument for or against the reality of cannibalism, or even a history of the subject, but rather as a casebook of some of the more notorious flesh-eaters in what we like to think of as the 'civilised' parts of the world. Instead of accounts from the jungles of Africa or the remote islands of the Pacific, herein will be found stories of people from Britain and Europe, America and China, who have all been irresistibly drawn to drink the blood and taste the flesh of their fellow human beings.

Most of these people, it transpires, have been driven by an impulse that is difficult to explain in rational terms – although man is by instinct, tradition and even choice a carnivore. Indeed, the fact is inescapable that there are very few types of creatures that exist on this planet that man has *not* eaten at one time or another.

The taboo which for years has surrounded the subject of man eating man how now thankfully been lifted in our more enlightened times, and only by studying the facts can a more complete and balanced picture of the phenomenon of cannibalism be made available. In the pages which follow are some histories which I submit should be taken as a part of the evidence . . .

The Legend of Ethne the Dread

In the British Isles, the earliest detailed account of
an individual who regularly ate human flesh
occurred in the third century AD. The dubious distinction of being the first British cannibal belongs
not to a man, but a remarkable female named
Ethne the Dread who was born in Wales some time
during the latter part of that century. She was, in
fact, of Irish extraction, her name being derived
from that of Eochhaidh Feidhleach, a mythological
Celtic hero, who was cruelly drowned in her last
month of pregnancy by her jealous sister, Clothra.
Ethne's own life was to be similarly drenched in
blood . . .

Wales in the late third century was a bleak and
inhospitable country with a few communities scattered on the hills and in the dark valleys. Along
the coast were also to be found various settlements
– the majority belonging to the native Welshmen,
but one distinctive and especially well-fortified

community had been built by settlers from across the Irish Sea. It stood on the shore of Pembroke, facing across the turbulent sea towards the modern Waterford. The place was a stronghold of the Desi tribe which – according to a narrative written in the eighth century from which the facts of this story have been drawn – was at this time lead by a ferocious and deeply superstitious warrior named Crimthand, who would later perish at the hands of a supernatural woman on the feast of Samhain.

The Desi were an Irish clan who had lived for centuries in the province of Mide or Meath, and they feature in a story, *Inndardba inna n Desi* (The Expulsion of the Desi), which has been stylistically dated back to the third century. According to this legend, Cellach, a son of Cormac Mac Art, the High King of Ireland, had raped a niece of a Desi chieftain while riding through their territory. The chief had then tracked Cellach to Tara and when the boy denied his act, killed him in a fit of rage. In retribution, Cormac Mac Art expelled the Desi from his lands. Some of them fled to Munster and the rest sailed across the Irish Sea and 'after a voyage of many adverttures' settled in south Wales. In exile, each succeeding generation of Desi dreamed of the day when they might return to their homeland.

Crimthand, the latest of the Desi rulers, shared this dream too, though he and his people now lived well enough from plundering the surrounding districts. Indeed, it has been suggested that the taste for human flesh which his daughter was to develop may first have surfaced in the father himself, for he is said to have occasionally drunk the blood of enemies slain in battle in order to imbibe some of their strength.

At the time of the events we are interested in, Crimthand was enjoying a lull in his attacks against the native population and had just taken a second wife, Cuiniu. This woman was, in fact, the sister of his first wife, who had died in mysterious circumstances.

The first child born to Crimthand and Cuiniu was a girl whom they named Ethne. On the night she was born, a famous druid, Bri, the son of Bairchild, happened to be in the stronghold, and immediately pronounced on the baby's future, according to the ancient narrative. His words were to have a profound effect upon the new father.

'The maiden that has been born tonight, all the men of Ireland shall know her,' said Bri, 'and on account of this maiden her mother's kindred will seize the land on which they shall dwell.'

Crimthand at once saw the implications of the druid's words in regard to the Desi dream, and gave orders that his daughter was to be brought up to be as strong and brave as any man in the tribe. No effort was to be spared in order that she should fulfil her destiny and lead the tribe back to Ireland to reoccupy their land in Meath.

According to the words of the legend, 'When the Desi heard the story from the druid that it was through the power of the maiden that they would obtain their inheritance, they reared her on the flesh of little boys that she might grow quickly.'

Crimthand ordered that each family of the tribe who had more than two sons was to sacrifice the youngest so that his daughter could eat the boy's tender flesh. No one else was to share this grisly meal, however.

The records do not make it clear whether the flesh was cooked or eaten raw, but Ethne nonetheless flourished on her diet, which was supplemented with a drink made by mixing mead and blood. She was, it is said, unable to differentiate between the meat she ate and the animals slaughtered and cooked for the rest of the Desi. It is doubtful whether the girl tasted any vegetables at all during her childhood.

While off on raiding trips into what is now Carmarthen, Crimthand and his men often deliberately seized boy children from isolated settlements and returned with them still alive to the coast as further 'supplies' for his voracious daughter.

By her teens, Ethne had the physique of a man and had been trained by her father to wrestle and handle all manner of weapons. She was, not surprisingly, regarded with awe by all the members of the tribe and with terror by small male children.

'Her name became Ethne the Dread,' says the narrative, 'for the little boys dreaded her.'

The cannibal warrior queen lived until she was in her early twenties, and although the evidence suggests that she lead at least two expeditions to Ireland in order to fulfil her destiny, on each occasion the raiders were driven back and had to retreat to Wales once more.

Mystery about her later life surrounds the death of Ethne the Dread. One record states she was fatally wounded during a foray to Ireland and died on the return journey. Another, probably apocryphal, says that she actually choked to death on a tiny bone in the dismembered arm of an infant on which she was feasting . . .

The Rough Grey Dog-Man

The story of the earliest English cannibal is, surprisingly, to be found amongst the threads of myth and legend which make up the great romance of King Arthur and his Knights of the Round Table. According to these tales, Arthur was a chieftain who united the British tribes – the Cymri who had been driven into the West of England by the Saxon invaders – and in so doing became the champion not only of his people, but also of Christianity.

The tales of Arthur's exploits are surrounded by a halo of chivalry and heroics. He is supposed to have been born in Tintagel Castle in Cornwall and thereafter lived in Caerleon, Wales. From this base he maintained a stubborn opposition to the Saxon marauders, supported in his endeavours by a group of brave knights and the love of his beautiful wife, Guinevere. He also allegedly embarked on various quests, slew a number of supernatural creatures and conquered several lands. The King was finally betrayed by his wife and closest knight and fatally wounded at the Battle of Camlan. Thereafter – so the story goes – he was taken to the isle of Avalon where, as a hero, he became one of the immortals, and waits to be called again in the hour of his country's need.

Beneath these fables about the hero's life, there is certainly a substrata of truth – in particular concerning the Saxon oppressors who made life so appalling for the Britons under their merciless rule.

Of Arthur himself it seems probable that he was the most visible of the victorious battle-leaders against the Saxons and lived at some period during the sixth century. There are, though, no specific details of his battles or his triumphs against the pagan invaders. Much of the romantic literature which has subsequently grown up around him can be traced no further back than the twelfth century, and is considered by several historians merely to reflect earlier folk traditions and mythological concepts about hero kings possessing supernatural powers.

Amongst the Saxons in Britain at this period of history, however, was one extremely degenerate group about whom we know rather more. They were led by a man named Gwrgi Garwlwyd, which translates literally as 'The Rough Grey Dog-Man'. According to a Triad, a group of sixth-century Welsh stories, Gwrgi and his confederates were not only traitors to the British cause but cannibals as well. To quote from a translation of the

Historical Triads of the Isle of Britain, Third Series, No.45:

'There were three arrant traitors who were the cause that the Saxons took the crown of the Isle of Britain from the Cymri. One was Medrawd [Mordred] who with his men became one with the Saxons to secure himself the kingdom against Arthur; and by reason of that treachery many of the Lloegrwys [the British] became Saxons. Secondly, there was Aeddan the Traitor of the North who gave himself and his men, within the limits of his dominions, to become Saxons, so as to be enabled to maintain themselves in usurpation and depredation under the protection of the Saxons.'

The third of these men, the Triad indicated, made the other two pale into insignificance.

'He was Gwrgi Garwlwyd, who, after getting a taste for human flesh at the court of Edelfled, King of the Saxons, liked it so much that he would eat nothing but human flesh ever afterwards; and therefore he and his men united themselves with Edelfled, so that he used to make secret incursions among the nation of the Cymri to satisfy his degraded palate.

'Because of these three arrant traitors, the Cymri lost their land and their crown in Lloegria [England]; and if it had not been for these treacheries the Saxons could not have gained the island from the Cymri.'

Other Triads from the same era, which were first

translated in the middle of the last century, supply further information about the flesh-eating habits of 'The Rough Grey Dog-Man'. For when Gwrgi Garwlwyd and his men made their furtive incursions into the strongholds of the Britons – usually under the cover of darkness – they concentrated on snatching youthful victims.

'They took male and female of the young,' says one Triad, 'as many as Gwrgi Garwlwyd ate daily; and they devoured daily two bodies of the Cymri at their dinner and two at their supper. And soon all the lawless men of the nation of the Cymri hastened to him and the Saxons where they obtained their fill of prey and spoil from the natives of this Isle.'

Descriptions of these cannibals and their prey indicate that the men only stunned their victims when capturing them and then kept them alive until they wanted to eat them. On some occasions, limbs would be literally torn from bodies while the victims were still alive in order that the roasted meat 'was of the freshest for their tables'.

There seems no doubt that Edelfled the Saxon ruler was an equally bloodthirsty cannibal, although there is only one specific report to support this claim:

'Edelfled, the King of Lloegria, required every night two noble maidens of the nation of the Cymri and violated them. The following morning he slew them and ate them.'

Small wonder, then, that this cannibal lecher

should have approved of 'The Rough Grey Dog-Man' marrying his sister, as another Triad informs us:

'Gwrgi Garwlwyd was married to the sister of Edelfled and committed treachery and murder conjointly with Edelfled upon the nation of the Cymri. Gwrgi killed a male and a female of the Cymri daily and devoured them. And on the Saturday he killed two of each, so that he might not kill on the Sunday.'

There are few more bizarre twists in the history of flesh-eating than the idea of a Sabbatarian cannibal – and it has been suggested that a Saxon with a weaker stomach or marginally more delicate sensitivities had tried to curb the man's excesses by suggesting he should 'keep holy the Sabbath day'. Nonetheless, the 'The Rough Grey Dog-Man' still ate his cannibal feast every Sunday.

There is evidence that the meals Gwrgi and Edelfled and their followers shared in the Saxon court were not always peaceful, and quarrels over the choicest cuts were frequent occurrences. Flesh from the tender bodies of young girls was regarded as the sole preserve of the highest ranks, the rest had to make do with the meat and bones of boys and adults.

The cannibal pursuits of both Gwrgi and Edelfled were finally brought to an end at the hands of assassins. Another Triad states that it was two brothers, the sons of a bard with the singular name of Dysgyvedawg – meaning Learning-drinker –

who killed the pair, though whether together or on separate occasions is unknown. The legend merely indicates that Edelfled was killed by 'Ysgavnell, the son of Dysgyuvedawg' while Gwrgi 'was slain by Difedel, the son of Dysgyvedawg'. Soon their memories would be almost completely obliterated by the fame of the Cymri warrior Arthur, who had so vigorously opposed them.

However, a curious rumour persisting for years after they were dead, which said that their bodies were actually eaten by some of those other Saxons who had not long before shared their cannibal feasts, seems to be without any foundation whatsoever . . .

The Monster of East Lothian

A cave at the foot of a spectacular, towering cliff known as Bennane Head on the Ayrshire coast, which faces out across the Firth of Clyde towards the rocky bird haven of Ailsa Crag, is the unlikely location of the most notorious cannibal legend in the British Isles – the story of Sawney Beane, also known as 'The Man-Eater of Scotland' and 'The Monster of East Lothian'.

The cave in which this flesh-eater and his in-bred family of forty-seven are said to have slaughtered and consumed over one thousand victims during a period of twenty-five years is to be found about three miles north of Ballantrae – but is far from easy to approach as it is accessible only by way of a very steep path. Yet such is the notoriety of the spot that numbers of curiosity seekers have been drawn to the coast over the years to view what is surely the grisliest 'tourist attraction' in the history books. Its notoriety has been further heightened by the fact that in 1977 a man fell and broke his back while navigating the path; and the same route has also taken the life of a boy trying to climb down the cliff.

Scotland – many parts of which were for centuries as wild and lawless as the remoter regions of continental Europe – has, in fact, something of a tradition in cannibalism.

As far back as AD 367, for example, a tribe of Scots known as the Attacotti, who lived in Argylshire, were notorious for eating other people – friends and foes alike. Not surprisingly, they struck fear into the hearts of North Britons whenever they made raids across the border into England. Sometimes they were in the company of other Scots, or else with gangs of Picts, Saxons or Franks. Apparently, the Attacotti did not leave the bodies of their fallen enemies or their own men to rot on the battlefields, but took away all they could carry for consumption later. According to the legend, these cannibals later gave up flesh-eating and, as a result of their reputation as fearless warriors, many were enrolled in the Roman Army as mercenaries!

'The Wild Men of Galloway' were another group of savage and warlike people who misused corpses in bestial ways at the time of the Norman invasion of England. 'They were not men,' says an account, 'but brute beasts, devoid of humanity.' These men frequently raided surrounding areas to carry off young men and women – some

24

of whom they are said to have used in trading with the Irish for cattle, while the tastiest were roasted for eating.

So when Sawney Beane began his reign of terror in the early years of the fifteenth century he was, to some, merely continuing the old ways. Yet such was the cruelty and bloodthirstiness displayed by Beane and his incestuous clan that they soon came to overshadow all the stories of the Attacotti and the other Scottish cannibals. The facts of his life and career certainly do not make pleasant reading.

There are several accounts of the life of Sawney – or Alexander (Sandy) – Beane, though most derive from a book published in 1700 by a historian named Captain Alexander Smith and fulsomely entitled, in the manner of the day, *A Compleat History of the Lives and Robberies of the Most Notorious Highwaymen, Footpads, Shoplifters and Cheats of both sexes in and about London and Westminster, and All Parts of Great Britain for above One Hundred Years past and Continued to the Present Time*. The facts concerning the Scottish cannibal and his bloody career as given by Captain Smith are these:

Sawney Beane was born in the county of East Lothian about eight or nine miles from Edinburgh in the year 1390. It has been suggested that his birthplace was the small town of Tranent, but this has proved impossible to substantiate as there are no census records in existence for that period in time. It is known that his parents worked as hedgers and ditchers, however, and apparently raised their son to follow in this occupation. The boy, though, had different ideas.

'Being very prone to idleness,' says Captain Smith's account, 'and not caring to be confined to any honest employment, he left his father and mother, and ran away into the desert part of the country.'

Sawney did not travel alone, however, but took with him a young woman 'as viciously inclined as himself', and after wandering the countryside for several months, the pair finally settled in the cave at Bennane Head. This cave was about seventy feet deep and wide at the mouth, and, according to archaeological evidence, had been occupied as early as the Stone Age.

Sawney Beane and his consort soon settled into the cave and were to remain there for the next twenty-five years, 'without ever going into any city, town or village,' Captain Smith says. Because he was too lazy to grow crops or even rear cattle – and cattle-rustling was then the most dangerous crime on the statute books, carrying a mandatory death penalty – Sawney decided that catching and eating people was preferable.

'In this time they had a great number of children and grandchildren,' the report continues, 'whom they brought up after their own manner, without any notions of humanity or civil society.

They never kept any company, but among themselves, and supported themselves wholly by robbing. Being, moreover, so very cruel that they never robbed anyone whom they did not murder.'

The Beane family grew rapidly on its unnatural diet of human flesh. Sawney and his 'wife' apparently had eight sons and six daughters, and they in turn produced eighteen grandsons and fourteen granddaughters, all of whom were taught to help in the waylaying of travellers, slaughtering them, and then returning quickly with the corpses to their isolated and well-hidden cave.

'The place which they inhabited was quite solitary and lonesome.' says Captain Smith, 'and, when the tide came up, the water went near two hundred yards into their subterraneous habitation, which reached almost a mile underground. So that when people, who were later sent armed to search all the places about, passed by the mouth of the cave, they never took any notice of it, never supposing any human being would reside in such a place of perpetual horror and darkness.'

Although no contemporary account exists of life at Bennane Head, a nineteenth-century historical novelist, S R Crockett, who was born in Laurieston in 1859 and grew up in the area where the story was a part of local tradition, later utilised some of the details in his novel, *The Grey Man*, published in 1896. In its pages he provides this vivid and probably reasonably accurate portrait of Sawney Beane and his tribe:

'They were of both sex and all ages, mostly running naked, the more stalwart of them armed with knives and whingers, or with knotted pieces of tree in which a ragged stone had been thrust and tied with sinews or tags of rope. The very tottering children were striking at one another, or biting like wolves, till the blood flowed. In the corner sat an old bleared hag, who seemed of some authority over them, for she pointed with her finger and the uproar calmed itself a little. The shameless naked woman-crew began to bestir themselves, and heaped broken driftwood upon the floor to which presently a light was set.'

Crockett described the leader of this appalling tribe in these words:

'Then Sawney Beane strode into the midst of the den. It happened that by misadventure he stumbled and set his foot upon a lad of six or seven, judging by the size of him, who sprawled naked in the doorway. The imp squirmed round like a serpent and bit Sawney Beane in the leg, whereat he stooped and catching the lad by the feet, he dashed his head with a dull crash against the wall, and threw him quivering like a dead rabbit into the corner. The rest stood for a moment aghast. But in a trice, and without a single one so much as going to see if the boy was dead or only stunned, the whole hornet's nest hummed again, and the place was filled with a stiffling smell of burning fat and roasting victual.'

In what is undoubtedly a remarkable piece of writing for a Victorian author steeped in the tradition of avoiding giving offence to the sensibilities of his readers, Crockett – through the eyes of his narrator – even offers a glimpse of the evidence of cannibalism to be seen all around Sawney Beane's cave.

'The cavern was very high in the midst,' he writes, 'but the sides not so high – rather like the sloping roof of an attic which slants quickly down from the rooftree. But that which took my eye amid the smoke were certain vague shapes, as it had been the limbs of human beings, shrunk and blackened, which hung in rows on either side of the cave. At first it seemed that my eyes must certainly deceive me, for the reek drifted hither and thither, and made the rheum flow from them with its bitterness.

'But after a little study of these wall adornments, I could make nothing else of it, than that these poor relics, which hung in rows from the roof of the cave like hams and black puddings set to dry in the smoke, were indeed no other than the parched arms and legs of men and women, who had once walked upon the upper earth – but by misfortune had fallen into the powers of this hideous, inconceivable gang of monstrous man-eaters.'

According to Captain Alexander Smith in his earlier report, the Beane tribe flourished in their sea-shore hideaway for a quarter of a century.

'By the bloody method of killing every victim, and by being so retired from the world, they continued for a long time undiscovered,' he records, 'there being no person able to guess how the people were lost that went by the place where they lived. As soon as they had robbed any man, woman or child, they used to carry off the carcass to the den, where cutting it into quarters, they would pickle the mangled limbs, and afterwards eat it, this being their only sustenance.

'And notwithstanding, they were at last no numerous, they commonly had superfluity of this their abominable food, so that in the night-time they frequently threw legs and arms of the unhappy wretches they had murdered into the sea, at a great distance from their bloody habitation. But the limbs were often cast up by the tide in several parts of the country, to the astonishment and terror of all beholders and others who heard of it.'

As the numbers of people who disappeared on the Ballantrae coastal road grew ever larger, wise travellers began to shun the route. Yet still the number of inexplicable deaths continued as a result of the Beanes roaming ever further afield in search of victims. With each new disappearance the public outrage grew stronger – the relatives and friends of those who were lost adding their voices to the clamour demanding to know what could have happened. Yet as year followed year the solution still seemed no nearer to hand.

'All the people in the adjacent parts were alarmed at such an uncommon loss of their neighbours.' the Smith account goes on, 'for there was no travelling in safety near the den of these wretches. This occasioned spies to be frequently sent into these parts, many of whom never returned again and those who did, after the strictest search and enquiry, could not find how these melancholy matters happened.

'Several honest travellers were also taken up on suspicion and wrongfully hanged upon bare circumstance. Several innocent inn-keepers were executed, for no other reason than that persons, who had thus been lost, were known to have lain in their houses, which occasioned a suspicion of their being murdered by them and their bodies privately buried in obscure places to prevent a discovery. Thus an ill-placed justice was executed with the greatest severity imaginable in order to prevent these frequent, atrocious deeds. So it was that many inn-keepers who lived on the western road of Scotland left their business for fear of being made examples of and followed other employments.'

The reign of terror which Sawney Beane and his family instituted and carried out with such precision seemed destined to defy all the efforts of the local magistrates to bring it to a halt. As well as the inn-keepers, many ordinary men and women living along the Ayrshire coast similarly began to fear for their lives and not a few fled northwards to Ayr, Kilmarnock and even Glasgow, leaving their homes empty behind them. Soon there was a very real fear that the whole coast might end up being depopulated if the mystery was not solved.

The Beane family grew, if anything, more daring in their ambushes. Even travellers who nursed the hope that there might be safety in numbers and journeyed in groups of half a dozen and more still fell victim to the cannibals. Because of their numbers, the family had no fear about attacking whole parties – though they always ensured that the ambush was carefully laid so that no one could escape to tell the story of what had happened.

If anything was going to stop Sawney Beane, it seemed, it would have to be pure chance. And so it proved, in the year 1435, as Captain Smith relates in grisly detail:

'A rider, with his wife behind him on the same horse, was coming home one evening from a fair when they were fell upon by these merciless wretches in a furious manner. The man, to save himself as well as he could, fought very bravely against the cannibals with sword and pistol, riding some of them down by the force of his horse. During the conflict, the poor woman fell from behind her husband and was instantly butchered before his face. The female cannibals cut her throat and fell to sucking her blood with as great a gusto as if it had been wine. This done, they ript up her belly and pulled out her entrails.'

Almost fainting with nausea at the sight of this apparent vampirism, the man nevertheless battled on against overwhelming odds – and just at the moment when he thought all was lost, a party of some twenty horsemen who were also returning from the fair happened to ride into the clearing. Even Sawney Beane knew these numbers were too much for him, and for the first time in their grisly career he and his family turned tail and fled back to Bennane Head.

'The brave horseman, who was the first ever to come off alive from an encounter with Sawney Beane, told the whole company what had happened,' explains Captain Smith, 'and showed them the horrid spectacle of his wife, whom the murderers had dragged to some distance, but had not time to carry her entirely off. They were all struck with stupefaction and amazement at what he related. They took him with them to Glasgow and told of the affair to the magistrates of that city, who immediately sent to the King concerning it.'

The appalling truth about what had occurred to the disappearing travellers on the Ayrshire coast now became apparent. According to some accounts, the King himself – King James I of Scotland – actually led a party of some four hundred men to try and locate the hideaway of the cannibals. More likely, he gave immediate orders for a search to be instigated and asked to be kept fully informed of developments.

Once again, fate was to play a hand in finally bringing the cannibals to justice. At the head of the large party was the man who had had the lucky escape from the Beane clan. And accompanying them all were a number of bloodhounds to ensure that every nook and cranny in the neighbourhood was thoroughly searched.

'No sign of any habitation was to be found for a long time.' Captain Smith's account continues, 'and even when they came to the wretches' cave they took no notice of it, but were going to pursue their search along the sea-shore, the tide being then out. But some of the bloodhounds luckily entered the Cimmerian den, and instantly set up a most hideous barking, howling and yelping, so that the searchers came back and looked into it.

'They could not conceive that any human could be concealed in a place where they saw nothing but darkness. Nevertheless, as the bloodhounds increased their noise they went farther in, and refused to come back again. Torches were immediately sent for, and a great many men ventured in, through the most intricate turnings and windings, till at last they arrived at that private recess from all the world which was the habitation of these monsters.'

The reaction of the party to the sights which they saw in the cave can only be guessed at. For there they found row upon row of legs, arms, torsos, hands and feet which had belonged to men, women and children, all hanging for the walls like so many joints in a butcher's shop. There were also great piles of clothing and mounds of jewellery, rings and gold and silver coins. Most revolting of all to be glimpsed in the flickering light of the torches were other limbs lying preserved in pickle . . .

Sawney Beane and his incestuous tribe made a last struggle for freedom, throwing themselves on the search party, biting, scratching and gouging in the terrible gloom of the cave. But the sheer weight of numbers and the pent-up rage of the searchers gave them the will to overcome the family. They were roped and bound together and soon began the long trek through the valleys of Ayr and Lanark to Edinburgh and justice. Before leaving the cave, the searchers gathered up all the human remains they could find and buried them in the sands outside.

News of the capture of the cannibal family preceded the filthy and bloodstained group, and hundreds gathered along the route to curse and hurl projectiles at them as they passed by. Only the protective ranks of the King's men prevented the local people from dispensing their own rough justice.

For one night Sawney Beane and his 'family' were kept under close guard in Edinburgh's Tolbooth and the following day they were escorted to Leith. Here, without even a semblance of a trial, they were all executed, 'it being thought needless to try creatures who were such professed enemies of mankind.'

Captain Alexander Smith provides the last gruesome paragraph in the history of Scotland's infamous cannibal family.

'At their execution, the men had first their privy members cut off and thrown into the fire, before their faces and their hands and legs were severed from their bodies, by which amputation they bled to death in a few hours. The wife, daughters and grandchildren having been made spectators of this just punishment, inflicted on the men, were afterwards burnt to death in three fires. They all in general died without the least signs of repentance, but continued cursing and venting the most dreadful imprecations to the very last gasp of life.'

The Madness of Christie O'
The Cleek

Sawney Beane was not, in fact, Scotland's only widely-known cannibal in the fifteenth century. A similarly bloodthirsty young rogue and his family also preyed on unsuspecting travellers on the east coast of Scotland in a manner that might well have been copied from the infamous Beane clan in the west.

In this instance, too, the cannibals lived in a cave not far from a picturesque little village called St Vigeans, which nestled in the shadow of the Sidlaw Hills not far from the outskirts of the fishing port of Arbroath. From this well-hidden retreat, the leader of the group was able to forage for victims in the Angus countryside: going as far inland as Forfar, and north as far as Montrose, and Carnoustie in the south. He is said to have killed several of his victims in the vicinity of the colourfully named 'Devil's Head', now a popular camping and caravanning centre on the coast just above Arbroath.

The real name of this man was long since been lost in the mists of time, but local tradition refers to him as Christie o' the Cleek and says that he was carrying out his barbarous practices around the middle years of the fifteenth century. The name probably referred to the locality in which the cave was located, while Christie is familiar as both a Christian name and surname in the braes of Angus.

Be that as it may, the most detailed account of Christie's depredations are to be found in a massive tome, *The Chronicles of Scotland – 1436-1565*, written by the remarkable if somewhat eccentric historian Robert Lindsay (c.1500-1565). Lindsay, who was born in Pitscottie, near Cupar, was fascinated by the history and legends of his native country, and although the style of his famous history is quaint and often garrulous, scholars are agreed that his facts, however graphically presented, are trustworthy. He apparently first heard about the Arbroath Cannibal during a trip along the east coast from Dundee to Aberdeen and followed up the details with some interest. He later described the facts as he had learned them with evident relish:

'About 1440 thair was ane briggant tane with his haill familie guho haunted a place in Angus.' Lindsay wrote in the *Chronicles*. 'This mischievous man

had ane execrable faschione to tak all young men
and childrene aither he could steall away quietlie,
or tak away without knawledge, and eat thame.
And the younger they war, esteemed them the
more tender and delitious.'

Christie o' the Cleek, as this mysterious figure
became known, was like Sawney Beane in that he,
too, left no trace of his victims to bear witness to
his methods. Indeed, it was not until after his capture that it was discovered he had devised a
unique method of stopping the victims he
ambushed on the road.

The ingenious Christie had fashioned himself a
hooked axe on the end of a long pole with which
he used to haul his victims from their horses as
they rode past his hiding place. Only the riderless
horses which later found their way to neighbouring places like Colliston or Kellie Castle bore witness to the disappearance of their owners, and
would, in time, lead to the attribution of at least
fifty victims to the cannibal.

Christie was apparently quite prepared to kill his
victims, but left the butchering and cooking of the
bodies to his wife. Some accounts of his life claim
that eating human flesh eventually turned him
mad, and made his actions increasingly unpredict-
able. Certainly, they finally lead to his capture.

It was in August 1460 that Christie was brought
to justice. He had apparently slaughtered a succession of victims in an area now known as Denhead
of Arbirlot on Elliot Water, which is just to the east

of Arbroath. These deaths had so aroused the local population that bands of vigilantes were set up and sent out into the district to try to track down the killer. The cannibal was said to have been sitting in his cave in St Vigeans when the search party finally caught up with him and surprised him and his family while they were actually eating a meal of human flesh.

Robert Lindsay describes the gruesome outcome of the arrest of Christie o' the Cleek in his inimitable narrative style:

'For his damnable abuse, he with his wayff and bairnes war all burnt, except ane young wench of a yeir old, who was saifed and brought to Dundee. She was here broucht up and fostered until she came to ane womanes years. She was then condemend and burnt quick for the same cryme.

'It is said,' Lindsay adds, 'that when she was cuming to the place of execution, thair gathered ane huge multitud of people, and speciallie of women, cursing hir that she was so unhappie as to committ so damnable deids. To which she turned about with an irefull countenance, saying, "Whyfore chyd yea with me as if I had committed ane unworthie act? Give me credance and trow me. If yea had experience of eating men and womanis flesch, yea wold think it so delitious that yea would nevir forbear it againe!"'

And having given this revolting show of bravado at her execution which took place before the

40

old Town House in the Seagate, says the chronicler, 'So bot ony signe of repentance, this unhappie traitour died in the sight of the people.'

The legend of Christie and his family continued to be common gossip in the area of Arbroath for years after their deaths. Perhaps understandably, the stories had had an impact on local homesteaders and travellers similar to the effect on those who had lived in Ballantrae while Sawney Beane was alive. Numbers of them left the St Vigeans area for fear the cannibalism might continue. Indeed, for a time the ghost of Christie o' the Cleek was reported to have been seen in the neighbourhood, occasionally joined in later years by a young woman who folk nervously suggested might be the daughter who had been burnt at the stake at Dundee.

But despite the novelty of his fearsome hooked axe and the number of his killings, there was seemingly not enough substance in Christie's story to preserve it as fully as that of his fellow cannibal in Ayrshire. Today he is little more than a footnote in the history of the county of Angus – though there are still those older members of the Christie families who give a little shudder at the suggestion of the cave in St Vigeans and the man who went mad there eating human flesh . . .

The Man-Eater of Clovelly

By one of those curious twists of fate, England's best-known cannibal also operated in a coastal locality. In this instance, the tiny, cliff-side village of Clovelly in Devon, with its single cobbled High Street known as 'Up-a-long' and 'Down-a-long', that plunges half a mile to the small harbour and shingle beach. It is a quite outstanding little community that has justifiably earned the description of being one of the country's showpiece villages.

In truth, exploring this enchanting place with its whitewashed, flower-bedecked cottages, all of which seem to be on the verge of tumbling down the tree-swathed cliffs, is rather like stepping back into an earlier century. Transport in and out of the village is on foot, while donkeys and sledges are used to carry provisions for the inhabitants. Though it has been in existence for over 900 years –

since before the days of the Domesday Book – Clovelly undoubtedly owes its present state of unspoiled charm to the Hamlyn family, who were the lords of the manor from 1738 and did much to preserve the village's unique beauty.

Yet, amidst all this beauty, there is a dark secret in Clovelly's past. A secret which many residents prefer to ignore – or pretend never happened. It is the legend of John Gregg and his family of 'Robbers, Murderers and Cannibals' who lived nearby, some four hundred years ago, and who story is recorded in a rare pamphlet first published in 1700 and of which only three copies are known to exist – one in the British Museum, one at Exeter University, and the third in Bideford Library, the nearest town to Clovelly, some nine miles to the west.

The prime reason why these residents are disinclined to believe the story of Gregg, who is said to have murdered and eaten hundreds of victims, is because of its uncanny similarity to that of Sawney Beane. They maintain it is simply the same tale transferred to their locality with the names changed. The reason *why* this should have been done is harder to explain, they admit, but one or two believe it might well have been the handiwork of an opportunist local chapbook publisher trying to create a bestseller in an age when sensation had to be really sensational to encourage the public to spend its hard-earned cash.

Yet on carrying out enquiries in Clovelly and making a study of the evidence to be found there, it seems to me that there is every possibility that the man *was* real and *did* carry out the bloody crimes of cannibalism of which he stands accused by history.

To reach the sea-shore at Clovelly where Gregg and his family had their hideaway involves – as it does for every visitor to the village – leaving your car in the park above the community and wandering down between the steep bank of cottages to the eighteenth-century curved stone quay and slipway which harbours the boats of lobster fishermen and holidaymakers. Within walking distance of here are the three localities which have been put forward as the 'home' of the Gregg family.

The first is a cavern only about 400 yards west of the jetty which, though perhaps a little too close to the community to offer total secrecy, is certainly deep and undoubtedly penetrates a long way into the cliffs. The second is a shaft known as Dingle Hole some two miles to the east, situated just off Hobby Drive – a walkway which links the village by way of some delightful woodlands to Hobby Lodge on the A39 road to Bideford.

The third cave is, for my money, the most probable both because of its remoteness and the fact that its depths are virtually unmeasurable and its passageways impenetrable to those who do not know them. This is at Mouth Mill, almost three miles due west of the harbour. Past it on the headland runs an ancient cliff path which leads to the only other important settlement on this part of the coast, Hartland Point. This towering mass, 325 feet high – which was known to the Romans as the 'Promontory of Hercules' – has a coastguard lookout point forever pounded by the Atlantic waves and is linked to Hartland Quay, where in the sixteenth century three of the nation's greatest sailors, Sir Francis Drake, Sir Walter Raleigh and Sir John Hawkins, financed the building of a small harbour. Even before this, Hartland was a focal point for travellers from all over Devon, who would have provided ideal victims for a criminal such as John Gregg. Another interesting point about Mouth Mill is that not far from here is the ancient Iron Age fort of Clovelly Dykes, which has given up evidence of human remains.

The pamphlet history of the Clovelly cannibal tells us that he was born near the city of Exeter during the early years of the fifteenth century. He was an idle and dissipated lad from his childhood, and there is a suggestion that he left home to join in the smuggling trade which was then rife along Bideford Bay where Clovelly is situated. As local historian Muriel Gorman has pointed out in her excellent book, *Old Bideford and District*, the port imported more tobacco than any other in the country and was a natural target for the smugglers who swarmed like a plague all along the Bristol Channel. The island of Lundy in the Channel was probably the centre of the running of their contraband, and as Clovelly was the nearest point to the island on the mainland the connection was an easy enough one for even a simple lad like John Gregg to make.

Smuggling was, though, a dangerous occupation, carrying the death penalty, and it may well not have been long before it occurred to young Gregg that robbing and murdering lone travellers on the mainland was a potentially less dangerous and perhaps more lucrative trade. And by disposing of the bodies by eating them, he and his common-law wife – whom he had apparently met in Exeter and brought to the coast with him – might hope to avoid detection and capture.

According to the pamphlet, the Greggs quickly spawned a family of equally vicious sons and daughters who, incestuously, then bred more children to help in the bloody trade being carried out along the coastal road under the cover of darkness. Like Sawney Beane in Scotland, John Gregg was said to have prospered in his secret hideaway for the best part of a quarter of a century, and during this time was never seen by another man or woman who lived to tell the tale.

The evidence suggests that the Greggs also amassed a great fortune in stolen valuables. And apart from eating the flesh of the victims, they preserved what they could not immediately make use of in brine, disposing of the offal and bones in the sea. The leaflet continues:

'John's family was at last grown very large, and every branch, as soon as able, assisted in perpetrating their wicked deed which they followed with impunity. Sometimes they would attack four, five or six footmen together, but never more than two on horseback. They were also very careful none should escape, an ambush being set up on every side to secure them in every way. How then was it possible that they should be detected when no one that saw them ever perceived anybody afterwards?'

The report added the information that the number of people they destroyed and ate was never calculated. Like Sawney Beane, however, it was an attack on a man and woman returning home from a visit – to Hartland Point in their case – which led to their downfall. Although the unfortunate woman was seized and butchered by the cannibals, the man escaped the same fate when some other travellers unexpectedly came across the struggle and helped him to beat off Gregg and his tribe.

The pamphlet says of the rescued man: 'He then told the company what had happened and shewed them the mangled body of his wife. They were struck with amazement and went and made it known to the Mayor of Exeter. In a few days a large party of men set out for the place where the tragedies were acted in order to find this hellish crew which for so long had been a nuisance to that part of the Kingdom.'

Aided like the searches in Scotland with hounds, this force finally tracked the cannibals to their cave near Clovelly. Here they found all the evidence of the family's gruesome appetites, with limbs hanging in rows along the walls and pieces of flesh preserved in brine.

'After their arrest, the whole family were conducted under a strong guard to Plymouth where they were executed without any process,' says the pamphlet. Like Sawney Beane, John Gregg also showed no remorse whatsoever at his actions and died cursing the assembled crowds who had come to see him and his family burned to death.

The similarities between the stories of the Scottish and English cannibals are certainly quite striking. But not so similar, I would suggest, as to validate the claim that the Gregg family were a fraud invented by a pamphlet writer. The evidence of cave-dwelling in the vicinity, the strength of the tradition in the neighbourhood, and the name of the Gregg family, which is a familiar one in Devon, point to more than a phantom murderer.

The Man-Eater of Clovelly is, in fact, long overdue the research and attention that has been given to his more famous cousin north of the border . . .

The Man Who Was Bluebeard

Although over the centuries Europe has spawned many bloodthirsty tyrants and cruel despots, Gilles de Rais, who was for a time the Baron Marshal of France and a comrade-in-arms of Joan of Arc but is today best remembered as the legendary Bluebeard, far surpasses them all with his record of slaughter, perversion, blood-drinking and cannibalism. Described rather euphemistically in some histories as a man of 'unnatural appetites', he is said to have performed occult ceremonies to raise the Devil and murdered as many as eight hundred children in order to use their blood and flesh for alchemy.

The popular version of the legend of Bluebeard portrays him as a man who had many wives and, losing interest in them, murdered them one after another and concealed the bodies. There even evolved a diluted tale for children wherein Bluebeard was an Eastern potentate, taking seven brides, all of whom mysteriously disappeared after their honeymoon. Finally, it was said, he took one wife too many and just as he was about to murder her too, was caught in the act and himself killed by his new bride's two courageous brothers, who had suspected the fate of their sister's predecessors.

In fact, the story of the real Bluebeard is far more ghastly than either the legend or the fairy-tales – for the original was a man whose passion was not for brides but for virginal young girls and boys.

To the world in general in the early years of the fifteenth century, Baron de Rais seemed a paragon of virtue. Born of noble parentage in 1404, he became one of the richest men in Europe when his father died while he was still in his teens. His fortune was enormously increased when he married the fabulously wealthy Catherine de Thouars, and then, to crown his achievements, de Rais was made Marshal of France and played a distinguished part in fighting against the English.

His life changed irrevocably, however, when Charles VII became king in 1422, succeeding his father, the ill-fated Charles 'the foolish', who lost the battle of Agincourt and went insane. Gilles de Rais decided to retire from public life to one of his estates at Tiffauges, where his enormous wealth and the unquestioning loyalty of his servants enabled his darker side to flourish in what became a constant orgy of cruelty and perversion.

De Rais lived like a king himself. He had a bodyguard of two hundred men, a private chapel of thirty canons, and an extensive library full of valuable and esoteric manuscripts. However, when all his riotous living and profligate expenditure seriously depleted his resources, he turned to alchemy to help him 'invoke devils and learn how to make gold', to quote a sixteenth century account of his bizarre life.

'He adored and sacrificed to spirits,' the report states, 'conjured them and made others conjure them, and wished to make a pact with the said evil spirits, and by their means to have and receive, if he could, knowledge, power and riches.'

To help him in his objectives, Gilles employed a number of alleged scholars in the occult – including Gilles de Sille, a renegade priest, and Jean de la Rivière, an unashamed mountebank – most of whom were frauds and did little but help to deplete his wealth still further. In 1439, for instance, a newcomer named Father Francesco Prelati from Florence joined a group of three other Italian dabblers in scorcery already in residence at Tiffauges and together they organised for de Rais a series of terrifying seances to try and raise a demon they named Baron.

'As failure followed failure,' states another account of Gilles de Rais' life, 'Father Prelati turned to rarer materials to cajole the spirits, especially young children, whose blood he said propitiated the devils and whose bones became magic powders.'

Although de Raise could easily enough conceal

his nefarious activities behind the high walls of his castle, rumours of his evil ways soon began to spread about the surrounding countryside. The stories became wilder and more terrible when a number of parents started to report that their children had gone missing after last being seen in the vicinity of the castle. It was whispered that the Baron was sexually abusing young boys and girls and then afterwards killing them. He was even said to be drinking the blood of the most comely.

The full enormity of what Bluebeard – as de Rais was nicknamed because of the strange colouring of his small beard – had committed did not come to light until charges were finally initiated against him in 1440. These charges, forty-seven in all, were laid by the Bishop of Nantes, Jean de Malestroit, to the Inquisitor General of France, Guillaume Merici. Although there seems little doubt that the Bishop harboured a deep-seated grudge against the master of Tiffauges due to an earlier dispute they had had over money, the long list of complaints he presented was as horrifying and disgusting as anything put before the notorious French Inquisition during its entire history.

A typical charge amongst these indictments against de Rais – all of which are couched in a mixture of legal jargon and emotional outpourings – reads as follows:

'According to initial reports of public gossip, resulting in a secret inquiry by the Right Rev. Bishop of Nantes, in his town and diocese, by the agents of the Deputy Inquisitor, and by the Prosecutor of the ecclesiastical court, into the following charges, all crimes and offenses governed by ecclesiastical law, and according to the lamentable outcries, tears and wailings, denunciations coming from many persons of both sexes, crying out and complaining of the loss and death of children, the aforesaid Gilles de Rais accused, and his accomplices, have taken innocent boys and girls, and inhumanly butchered, killed, dismembered, burned and otherwise tortured them; and the said Gilles, accused, has immolated the bodies of the said innocents to devils, invoked and sacrificed to evil spirits, and has foully committed the sin of sodomy with young boys and in other ways lusted against nature after young girls, spurning the natural way of copulation, while both the innocent boys and girls were alive and sometimes dead or even sometimes during their death throes.'

Other charges referred to Gilles de Rais pouring the blood and pieces of flesh of children into a glass vessel and, after having tasted this, 'offering it to the demon Baron, in sign of his homage and tribute.' Following these depraved rituals, said a further statement, the accused 'had the bodies of the innocents burned, and the remains thrown in the trenches and ditches of the said castle.'

The court which began sitting to hear the evidence against Bluebeard on 13 September – at which he was present, apparently having appeared of his own free will – was offered a deluge of evidence from parents who claimed to have lost children last known to have been going to Gilles de Rais' castle. The deposition of one Thomas Aysee may be taken as typical of many more:

'Thomas Aysee and his wife, living at St Peter's Gate, go on record under oath that they are poor folk and about last Easter they had sent their son, aged about ten years, to seek alms at the castle where the Sire de Rais was then, and that since that time they have not seen the said child nor had news of him. Except that the wife of the aforesaid Aysee said that a little girl, whose name nor parentage she does not know, had told her she had seen her son at the almsgiving at the said castle, and that alms had first been given to the girls and then after to the boys. This little girl said she had heard that one of the people belonging to the castle said to the son of the aforementioned Aysee that he had no meat, but that if he went to the said castle, he would have some, and that after this conversation he had entered the castle and was seen no more.'

Evidence was also given to the court by two of Gilles de Rais' personal attendants, Henry Griart, aged twenty-six, and Etienne Poitou, aged twenty-two, both of whom stated that after their master had debauched the children they were all killed. Poitou claimed himself to have counted between thirty-six and forty-six heads of dead children.

The younger man's testimony continued with

more specific statements that Gilles de Rais often masturbated while straddling the bodies of his small victims.

'After having had an orgasm on the stomach of the said children holding their legs between his,' said Poitou, 'he had considerable pleasure in watching the heads of the children separated from the body. Sometimes he made an incision behind the neck to make them die slowly, at which he became greatly excited, and while they were bleeding to death he would sometimes masturbate on them again until they were dead, and sometimes he did this after they had died while their bodies were still warm.'

This witness said that de Rais sometimes sucked the children's blood and would occasionally bite the breasts of the prettiest girls 'as if he meant to eat their very flesh'.

Both Poitou and Griart gave evidence that their master had an even more ghastly way of restraining the children during these orgies of blood and debauchery.

The court record of their testimonies reads: 'In order to stifle the cries of children when he wished to have relations with them, he would first put a rope round their neck, and hang them up three feet off the floor in a corner of the room, and just before they were dead he would cause them to be taken down, telling them they would not utter a word, and then he would excite his member, holding it in his hand, and afterward have an emission on their stomach. When he had done this, he had their throats cut and their heads separated from their bodies. Sometimes he would ask, when they were dead, which of these children had the most beautiful head.'

Gilles de Rais had sat silently while the testimonies were read and evidence was given by the procession of witnesses. At the conclusion, he was charged with being, 'a heretic, apostate and conjurer of demons' and of performing 'crimes and vices against nature, sodomy, sacrilege and violation of the immunities of the Holy Church'.

When at last invited to answer the charges, de Rais stood up and curtly dismissed them all as 'frivolous and lacking credit'.

But the Inquisition was clearly unimpressed by such a sweeping declamation – especially as they had now gone through six long and tiring sessions. On 21 October, the Inquisitor General ordered that de Rais should be tortured until he promised to confess 'voluntarily and freely', as the record of the proceedings puts it.

When the man known as Bluebeard was brought back into the court he was a shadow of his former self. Gone was his mood of contempt and instead there appeared a broken man, his features distorted with pain and his body bearing the evidence of having been torn on the rack. There were even vivid traces of blood smearing his beard.

In a faltering voice the Baron now agreed that he was guilty of all the charges. He confessed to having enjoyed his vice, taking particular pleasure from cutting off the heads of children with a dagger or a knife, and at other times beating the youngsters to death with a stick.

The court also heard him confess that he 'kissed voluptuously the dead bodies, gloating over those who had the loveliest heads and the most attractive limbs.' He said his greatest pleasure was to sit across their stomachs and watch them slowly pass away.

The crumpled figure then finished his statement with an appeal to 'the fathers and mothers of those I have so piteously slain to pray for me.' Quite unmoved by any of this, the court found him guilty on all the charges.

On 26 October 1440, the sentence of the law that he should be burned at the stake was carried out. Because of his 'confession' and his rank, de Rais was allowed to be strangled to death before his body was placed on the funeral pyre. His relatives were also given permission to remove the body before it was consumed by flames and bury it secretly in the grounds of a Carmelite church on the Baron's lands.

There was much that was irregular in the trial of Gilles de Rais – none of his servants other than Griart and Poitou was allowed to give evidence in his defence, and even a plea of mercy from some of the other French noblemen who had served with him in the campaigns against the English was not admitted by the court. Nor was anyone allowed to remind those sitting in judgement that just nine years and five months earlier, another warrior from those same battles had also gone unjustly to the stake – Joan of Arc.

That de Rais was a pervert with a blood fetish seems beyond doubt. But it is the murders of children and their actual numbers which continues to worry historians. De Rais had, though, achieved a place in history which continues to fascinate people to this day – whether as a character from fairy-tales or as a monster with a blue beard . . .

The Werewolf of Dole

On the busy main road in northern France which runs from Dijon to the Swiss border stands the solid old town of Dole. Picturesquely sited on the River Doubs in the Franche-Comté region, it has become a popular stopping place for numbers of tourists travelling south after they have struggled clear of the traffic of Paris and motored through the beautiful Champagne country.

But Dole is also a community that for a period in the sixteenth century was infamous as the prowl of a werewolf whose attacks on children reached epidemic proportions and caused a proclamation to be issued by the local authorities giving people the right to hunt down and, if necessary, kill, 'a werewolf who it has been said has already seized and carried off several little children'.

The tradition of the werewolf – or lycanthropy, meaning literally 'wolf-man' and derived from the Greek lukanthropia – is almost as ancient as the

59

presence of the wolf himself. Although the wolf is no longer a native of the British Isles, he did roam the country here for many centuries. In Europe, though, the animal has never disappeared and has always been particularly prevalent in France, Germany and Hungary. Here stories of the loup-garou, the werewolf and the vulkodlak are to be found in folklore and historical records from the Middle Ages right through to modern times.

In the earliest times, it was believed that a man could literally be transformed into a wolf at the time of the full moon and – rather like the vampire – wander the countryside looking for victims whose flesh he ate and whose blood he lapped. Before dawn, it was said, the werewolf would return to his normal shape and continue to live unnoticed among his neighbours.

However, unlike the vampire, which required a stake driven through the heart to be killed, it was believed by those who lived in fear of werewolves that they could be stopped by ordinary bullets. Certainly a specially-minted silver bullet was thought to be even more effective – and it is interesting to learn that in some parts of Europe as late as the eighteenth century it was firmly believed that the werewolf possessed a thick, bushy tail and this was one of the infallible tests doctors carried out on a suspect!

Today the salient features of lycanthropy are accepted to be hallucinations in which the sufferer has a sadistic craving for blood. At this time, the man (or woman, because there are some recorded instances of female werewolves) believes he has been turned into a wolf, wanders the countryside at night attacking people and devours their flesh, and then returns to human form. Few can remember their actions upon waking, beyond the horror of discovering blood on their hands and the conviction they may have savaged some innocent victim during the night.

Amongst all the European nations, France undoubtedly has the strongest werewolf tradition, with a large number of the stories centred on the lonelier mountain regions such as Burgundy, the Dordogne and the Auvergne. In fact, the belief still persists in places such as Normandy and Brittany, where tales can be heard of men who have put on wolf-skins after nightfall to assume the savage habits of the beast.

The sixteenth century was, however, the period when the belief in lycanthropy was at its most widespread in France, and it is also the time when the events of the well-documented case of Gilles Garnier, the Werewolf of Dole, reached their climax in 1574. Garnier was, though, to be accurate, merely the latest example in a whole series of outbreaks which had started – according to historical records – at Poligny in 1521 when three werewolves were caught actually eating their victims and publicly executed. They were followed by Jean Peyral who claimed to have had intercourse with a wolf in order to assume the shape of the creature;

and then Pierre Burgot and Michel Verdun who were burned alive at Besancon in 1552 for 'having danced and sacrificed to the devil, and having changed themselves into wolves and devoured children'.

The man Garnier was apparently a sullen and impoverished wretch who lived in a tiny hovel with a wife named Appoline. He was said to have come originally from Lyons and sustained himself and his wife by begging in the streets. It was said also that most local people around Dole preferred to give the couple a few sous or some vegetables to keep them away from their doorsteps. Familiar though the pair were in the area, few people ever gave them more than a passing glance of distaste . . .

It was in August 1573 that the horror of the were-wolf first manifested itself in the normally tranquil region of Franche-Comté.

Just before dawn on the morning of 24 August, a group of labourers were going into a pear orchard near the village of Perrouze. Suddenly ahead of them they saw what looked like a figure bending over the prostrate figure of a child. As one of the workman called out, the shape seemed to look up and then scuttle away into the undergrowth.

The men rushed forward and were appalled to discover the dead body of a twelve-year-old village boy who was known to several of them. His throat had been torn open, it seemed, by savage teeth.

When the men had recovered from their initial

shock, they naturally began to wonder what had caused the boy's brutal death. One man, who regularly went hunting, thought the shape they had seen was rather like that of a wolf – but though the figure had run away without seeming to rise on to two legs, there was also something human about it.

The party gently lifted the small corpse and carried it back to Perrouze. A distraught mother was found who had been waiting all night for her son to return home. At least that part of the mystery was solved. But what no one could answer was who – or *what* – had been the killer?

A week later the body of another child, a girl, was found on the outskirts of Dole at a place called Salvange. This time there was clear evidence that pieces of flesh had been stripped from the child and, possibly, eaten or taken away. When a third victim of the nocturnal killer, a boy aged ten, was discovered at Courchapon, the people of Franche-Comté began to believe that the stories of were-wolves which they had heard since their childhood might be more than a legend. It seemed as if they had one in their midst.

As word quickly spread of the three killings, other tales of attacks by a mysterious creature which had gone on through the summer also began to emerge. Apart from the children, some adults also claimed to have been the victims of assault by something of inordinate strength which had leapt upon them from the cover of darkness.

The creature was said to have scratched and clawed and given off the smell of damp fur.

The frightened and angry citizens at once demanded that the authorities take some action. And after a meeting of the local *parlement* on 13 September, the following proclamation was posted throughout the district:

'According to statements made to the sovereign court of the *parlement* at Dole, in the territories of Espagny, Salvange, Courchapon, and the neighbouring villages, has often been seen and met, for some time past, a werewolf, who it is said has already seized and carried off several little children, so that they have not been seen since.

'And since this werewolf has attacked and done injury in the country to some horsemen, who kept him off only with great difficulty and danger to their persons, the said court, desiring to prevent any greater danger, has permitted, and does permit, those who are abiding or dwelling in the said places and others, notwithstanding all edicts concerning the chase, to assemble with pikes, halberds, arquebuses and sticks, to chase and to pursue the said werewolf in every place where they may find or seize him; to tie and to kill, without incurring any pains or penalties.'

The edict provided the people of Dole with the mandate they required to set up a force of vigilantes and hunt down the werewolf. This they at once proceeded to do.

For several nights the band of hunters patrolled

the area, some on horseback and some of foot, but no sign of the marauding beast was seen. The fact that parents had been urged to keep a close watch on their offspring and not to permit them out of doors at night may well have contributed to this lull in the attacks. Indeed, during the rest of September and October, only a half a dozen cases were reported, and of these only one bore the same hallmarks as the earlier attacks.

Then on 9 November events took a dramatic turn. Just as night was falling, a small group of peasants arrived breathlessly in the village of Chestenoy with the torn and bleeding body of a little girl. The child was not dead, but deeply traumatised by her experience. She had been savagely bitten in five places.

According to one of the peasants, the girl was actually being mauled by a 'huge wolf' as they approached, and it had fled into the dusk as soon as they had approached. Stranger still, a couple of the men thought they recognised the wolf as having the features of the disreputable outcast Gilles Garnier.

On 15 November, another child, a ten-year-old boy, was reported missing by his mother. He had last been seen in the vicinity of Armanages.

Rumour and suspicion now began to mount against Garnier, who had been less visible of late begging for his livelihood. A group of the vigilantes, emboldened by the powers given to them by the local *parlement*, decided to ride to Garnier's hovel and arrest him and his wife for questioning.

The evidence as to whether Garnier immediately confessed to being a werewolf or was tortured into making a confession by the vigilantes or the court officials is far from clear. Suffice it to say that he and Appoline were swiftly brought to the court house at Dole and put on trial for practising lycanthropy.

The documents which still survive relating to the trial state that Garnier made a number of confessions which confirmed at least some of the accusations made against him. The first of these concerned the attack in the pear orchard at Perrouze. Garnier confessed that he had killed the young boy and then added a curious couple of sentences that mixed piety with cannibalism.

'I killed him with my claws,' said the recluse, 'and in spite of the fact that it was Friday, I wanted to eat his flesh. But I was prevented from doing so by the approach of some men.'

Garnier told the court that he had appeared as a man not as a wolf, a fact which the eyewitnesses, having had time to gather their thoughts, also agreed with.

However, on 6 October Garnier said he had 'taken the shape of a wolf' and attacked a ten-year-old girl in a vineyard near a wood known as La Serre, about a mile from Dole. He had killed her with his teeth and claws. What followed in his confession sickened everyone who was there to listen to it in court.

The old man said he had stripped the body of

the child naked and eaten her flesh. He said he had enjoyed the flesh so much that he had even taken some of it home to his wife.

There then followed a period of inactivity when the bands of men searching for Garnier had been at their most active – and he did not kill again until 9 November. Once more he took the shape of a wolf and struck down another girl in a meadow at La Poupée, between the villages of Authune and Chestenoy. Here he had been interrupted by three passersby just as he started feasting on the child's flesh and he had been forced to flee.

According to Garnier's evidence, his attacks grew more ferocious the more victims he encountered. The lust for blood and flesh which coursed through his veins, he said, made him know how the wolf felt when it pounced upon its prey.

November 15 proved to be the day of his final killing. At another locality not far from Dole between Gredisans and Menote he had again assumed the form of a wolf and strangled a ten-year-old boy. Garnier said he had torn the body limb from limb – severing one leg with his fangs and then eating the flesh of the belly and thighs.

No one in the court had ever heard such a confession before and the enmity towards the dirty and unkempt recluse was almost palpable. His matter-of-fact description of his appalling killings further incensed the parents of the dead children who had crowded into the court house to listen to the trial. The verdict of death was a foregone conclusion and was greeted by a wave of cheering which echoed throughout the streets of Dole, according to a contemporary account.

On 18 January 1574, Gilles Garnier was executed in the main square of the town at the very spot where he had for years sat begging for alms. He was burned alive at the stake without even being allowed the mercy of strangulation beforehand.

Whether the 'Werewolf of Dole' was a true lycanthrope who actually changed into a wolf before committing his killings, as he claimed, seems most unlikely. But of his appetite for cannibalism there can be no doubt – while the number of his victims also ranks him as one of France's worst serial killers.

The Bloody Countess

At the beginning of the seventeenth century, sinister reports began to filter through the Carpathian mountains and across the lowlands of Hungary about the discovery of the bodies of dozens of young girls, all of whom appeared to have died in agony before their bodies had been callously dumped. But that in itself was not what most horrified the peasants who stumbled across the corpses in their woods and fields – it was the fact that each and every one had been drained of all its blood.

The area in which these grisly remains were found is, of course, famous today as the setting of Bram Stoker's classic novel *Dracula*, and such an outrage might easily be ascribed to his vampirism – if, that is, Count Dracula had been a real person and not a figment of his creators imagination. In fact, the truth of this story is far more horrifying than any piece of fiction and exposed a human

69

monster obsessed with a belief that blood was the elixir of youth and beauty. An obsession so strong that as many as 650 innocent young girls may have been slaughtered in the pursuit of these objectives.

The perpetrator of these gruesome crimes was no ordinary lunatic, however, but a famous society beauty and a member of one of the most aristocratic families in Europe, someone who would subsequently go down in history as 'a blood-thirsty and blood-sucking Godless woman caught in the act at Csejthe Castle,' to quote one report. Her name was Countess Elisabeth Bathory and according to at least one expert on the supernatural she has the dubious distinction of being 'probably the only reliably recorded instance of vampirism in the annals of Europe'.

The Countess, variously known as 'The Terrible Ogress' and 'The Tigress of Csejthe', developed her obsession with the blood of young virgins when still a young woman and pursued it with single-minded cruelty and gruesome ingenuity throughout the rest of her life. She slaughtered young girls without conscience and drained them so she could drink the blood, or alternatively use it to bathe in 'blood-baths', and thus preserve her looks. To some literary historians this vampire lady of the Carpathians was the real inspiration for Bram Stoker's novel.

The discovery of those pale and emaciated corpses in the year 1611 led to an official enquiry which soon tracked down the culprit to the residence of the Bathory family: the imposing Csejthe

Castle situated in the Carpathian foothills. The scandal which resulted had such an impact on Hungarian society that a royal proclamation was handed down by King Matthias II that neither the Countess nor her crimes were ever to be mentioned in public. Indeed, it was to be almost two hundred years before the full enormity of her crimes was to become generally known in Europe and elsewhere.

An Austrian scholar, Michael Wagener, was the first to assemble the facts about the life of the Bloody Countess in his book, *Beitrage zur philosophischen Anthropologie*, published in 1796. He was also the first to explain how her obsession had begun.

Elisabeth Bathory was born in 1561 into a powerful, strongly Protestant, Hungarian family. Despite a strict upbringing, she quickly grew into a sexually adventurous girl with a streak of sadism in her character that developed rapidly once she had become a teenager. Perhaps already aware of her tendencies, Elisabeth's family arranged for her to be engaged at the tender age of eleven to the scion of another powerful family, Count Ferencz Nadasy. But this did nothing to inhibit her craving for peasant boys – and just before her fifteenth birthday she gave birth of a child, apparently fathered by one of these lads. A few months later, however, the infant was smuggled secretly out of the country and she was safely married to the Count at one of the biggest society weddings seen in the country for many years. Initially, says Michael Wagener, she tried to be a good wife to her new husband.

'Elisabeth was wont to dress well in order to please her husband and spent half the day over her toilet,' he states. 'Then on one occasion her chambermaid saw something wrong with her head-dress, and as a recompense for observing it, received such a severe box on the ears that blood gushed from her nose and spurted on to her mistress's face. When the blood drops were washed off the Countess's face, her skin appeared much more beautiful: whiter and more transparent on the spots where the blood had been.

'Elisabeth therefore formed the resolution to bathe her face and her whole body in human blood so as to enhance her beauty. Two old women and a certain fellow called Ficzko assisted her in her undertaking. This monster used to kill her luckless victims, and one of the old women caught the blood in which Elisabeth would bathe at the hour of four in the morning. After the bath she appeared more beautiful than ever.'

In the years that followed, the Countess exercised her sexual and sadistic whims at every opportunity. She clearly enjoyed inflicting pain, and was merciless on any serving girl who displeased her. And to amuse herself during her husband's long absenses from the castle while furthering his distinguished career in the Hungarian army by successfully fighting the Turks, she conducted endless heterosexual and lesbian orgies at which perversion of all descriptions were not only permitted, but encouraged.

Nothing, it seemed, worried Elisabeth Bathory, or disturbed the cruel tenor of her life. Certainly not what she saw as her undisputed right as an aristocrat to do as she chose with peasant girls whom she probably did not even regard as human beings. Nor did such behaviour run contrary to her religious beliefs or her duty to her husband and family (she had four children to whom she was apparently devoted). Nothing, that is, except the fear of losing her beauty.

When Count Bathory died in 1604, worn out by the demands of his military campaigning, the first chill winds of ageing were beginning to blow around Elisabeth. Now aged forty-three, middle age was starting to appear in the form of tiny wrinkles around her mouth and eyes. Even her magnificent dresses and fabulous jewels could not hide every flaw. Yet still her appetite for sex and new pleasures was undiminished, and realising she could not do without the flattery and attention of men, she redoubled her efforts to preserve her looks and attract new suitors.

To satisfy her need for fresh blood with its supposed curative powers, the Countess demanded still greater numbers of pretty young girls to be brought to the castle, and her faithful procurers were sent ever further afield to recruit victims. Only those who had 'not yet tasted the pleasures of love' were to be recruited, she insisted. Quite why so many parents allowed their daughters to be taken away, when Elisabeth's fearsome reputation was already common gossip and disappearance followed disappearance, is one of the mysteries of this bloody saga. Fear of the Barthorys may well have been the spur, but the fact remains that at the peak of her obsession, the Countess was killing and draining the bodies of these girls at the rate of at least five a week.

'The unhappy girls who were lured to the castle under the promise that they were to be taken into service there were locked up in a cellar,' Michael Wagener states in his report. 'Elisabeth not infrequently tortured the victims herself; often she changed her clothes, which dripped with blood, and renewed her cruelties.'

The methods which the Countess used to drain the blood of her victims for her cosmetic needs were many and varied. One such method, reported in the later trial record, was to 'put a terrified naked girl in a narrow iron cage furnished with pointed nails turned inwards, hang it from the ceiling, and sit beneath it enjoying the rain of blood that came down.'

A still more gruesome method was a robot known as the Iron Maiden which had been designed to her specification by a German clockmaker and installed in the castle cellars.

'Shaped like a naked girl and covered with blonde hair and wearing red teeth torn from the mouth of some servant, the automaton also had red nipples and public hair,' says a contemporary report. 'It had eyes that opened and closed like an attractive doll and, when set in motion, would clutch anyone that came near it in a tight embrace and then transfix them with a series of sharp points that came out of the metal breasts. Other concealed spikes also pierced the victim's genitals. The blood of the girls ran down into a channel so that it could be collected, warmed over a fire, and then used for the Countess's bath.'

In her obsession to preserve her youth, Elisabeth would also drink blood from the wounds and burn blisters of girls who were tortured and dying. To satisfy her perverted nature she sometimes even forced her victims to eat the flesh of their predecessors.

According to the Reverend Janos Ponikenusz, the Lutheran pastor of Csejthe, who was one of those who took part in the downfall of the Countess: 'We have heard at Csejthe from the very mouths of girls who survived the torture that some of their fellow victims were forced to eat their own flesh roasted on the fire. The flesh of other girls was chopped up fine like mushrooms, cooked and flavoured, and given to young lads who did not know what they were eating.'

Occasionally Elisabeth herself tasted flesh. Dorottya Szentes, one of her accomplices, who also later gave evidence against her mistress, said: 'When she was not feeling well and did not have the strength to beat anyone, she would draw one of the serving maids suddenly to herself and bite a chunk of flesh from her cheeks and sink her teeth into her breast and shoulders. She would also stick needles into a girl's fingers and say, "If it hurts you, you famous whore, pull them out," but if the girl dared to draw the needles out, her ladyship ordered her to be beaten and her fingers slashed with razors.'

Despite all her endeavours and the ever increasing toll of the murdered girls, Elisabeth could do nothing to halt the process of ageing. She was seemingly on the point of despair when one of her accomplices, a woman named Erzsi Majorova who had apparently provided her with a number of useful potions, suggested that it was not the blood which was failing her, but the *type* she was using. The blood of peasant girls could not possibly have the properties she needed: only the 'blue blood' of those of noble birth had the power to regenerate her beauty.

'This was not quite so easy,' Reay Tannahill, a social historian who has made a study of cannibalism in her book *Flesh and Blood* (1975), states, 'but in the winter of 1609, with macabre humour, the Countess arranged to accept twenty-five daughters of the minor nobility whom she was prepared to instruct in the "social graces". It was the beginning of the end. Explaining away the deaths or disappearances of numerous well-born girls was very different from merely shrugging off

the fate of peasants. And the Countess made another disastrous mistake. She had the bodies of
four naked girls tossed over the ramparts one
winter night when wolves were on the prowl, and
the villagers found them before the wolves did.'

The murmurs of discontent from those living in
the surrounding countryside now grew to a roar of
anger. At last a few brave souls had the courage to
stand up to the Countess and report what was
going on to the authorities in Vienna. The sheer
volume of unexplained deaths in the neighbourhood and the continuing gossip of terrible screams
being heard from the cellars of the castle night
after night gradually reached the ears of the King.
Then Pastor Ponikenusz smuggled to court a secret
message in which he listed in detail the horrors he
knew had been committed by Elisabeth and this
finally prompted action.

On 3 December 1610, Count Gyorsy Thurzo, the
governor of the province, who was also Elisabeth's
cousin, set out with a party of soldiers, *gendarmes*
and the village priest to raid the castle and arrest
everybody in it. According to later reports, the
men walked in to find themselves in the midst of
an orgy of blood.

In the main hall, they found the Countess herself *in flagrante delicto* with two men. Nearby was
the dead body of a girl drained of blood; another
still alive whose body had been pierced with tiny
holes; and a third evidently still being tortured. In
the dungeons and cellars below they came across a

77

number of other girls, some of whose bodies had already been pierced and – in the words of one of the rescuers – 'milked of their blood'. There were others still unharmed, 'plump, well-fed and like well-kept cattle in their stalls'. The dead bodies of fifty more were subsequently discovered in the most rudimentary graves.

The Countess herself arrogantly denied any knowledge of the deaths – and when her closest accomplices confessed their parts in the reign of bloodshed in the hope of saving their necks, she firmly laid the blame for any atrocities on them. As a member of the Hungarian nobility, she did not expect to be asked to account for any of her actions. Indeed, such were the laws of Hungary at that time that it would have taken an Act of Parliament to force her into any court of law.

As it was, the servants who had served her evil purpose were tried in the court of the nearby small market town of Bicse in January 1611 and all were ordered to be put to death. But Elisabeth did not escape retribution of a sort. King Matthias, being completely satisfied of her guilt though unable to exercise the death penalty, handed out the only appropriate sentence he could think of. She was to be walled up in Csejthe Castle for the rest of her life 'to repent her bestial ways'.

Subsequent reports state that the Countess was immured in a small room with the windows and door bricked over and only a hatch for food linking her to the outside world. For three and a half years

Elisabeth Bathory lived almost literally the existence of the 'vampire lady' that history now calls her – locked in the icy tomb of her castle. She died there on 14 August 1614.

For years after her death, the Castle remained empty – four gibbets at each corner a constant reminder to everyone who passed of the horrors which had been perpetrated within. Then, one night in the eighteenth century, in a scene reminiscent of those which so regularly form the climax of horror movies, it was struck by lightning and burned to the ground. Although no trace remains today, the name of Elisabeth Bathory, the 'Bloody Countess' is still spoken of in whispers and with a shudder of disgust by those who live in the bleak Carpathian mountains . . .

The Cannibal Troops

History has many tales of victorious soldiers who are said to have eaten the bodies of their fallen enemies, believing that by so doing they would take possession of the man's life-essence and vitality through the simple process of swallowing some of him. It is stated that Ancient Egyptian troops frequently cooked and ate the flesh of the bravest of their enemies, as did the Scythians from the Black Sea and many of the armies raised by the warlords of China during the various dynasties. To their number can be added the aborigines of Australia, the Maoris of New Zealand, the Hurons and Iroquois of America, the Ashanti of Africa and even the Uscochi people in the Balkans.

Closer to home, in Ireland around the twelfth century there were said to be several chieftains who regularly ate the flesh of vanquished enemies to demonstrate their total victory. A description of one of these chiefs in George Laurence Gomme's

Ethnology in Folklore (1892) says he, 'tore the nostrils and lips of the head of a man brought to him by his soldiers, using his teeth in a most savage and inhuman manner.'

In England, it was for many years believed that the wild Highland soldiers ate any children who fell into their hands. As late as 1745, there is evidence that when it was feared that Prince Charles's troops might be coming to raid England, 'children were sent out of the way for fear that the Highlanders should devour them.' to quote a report in *Notes & Queries* of 17 September 1887.

There is, however, no more extraordinary figure in the association between cannibalism and soldiering than Sir Thomas Lunsford, the Cavalier leader who was widely known as 'Bloodybones' and is alleged to have eaten the flesh of a number of plump children during the English Civil War. There is evidence to support this grisly accusation as well as counter-claims that it was all a Roundhead invention to frighten waverers to the cause.

The story of the struggle in the middle years of the seventeenth century between the King, Charles I, with his Royalist supporters, and the Parliamentarians lead by Oliver Cromwell, need take up no more than a few lines of background detail here. The war fell into two parts: the first began in August 1942 when Charles raised his standard at Nottingham, and ended in May 1646 when he surrendered. This period included the important battles of Edgehill (23 October 1642),

Marston Moor (2 July 1644) and Naseby (14 June 1645), the latter two of which were decisively won by the Roundheads. The second period was the Royalist and Presbyterian rising of March to August 1648 which was also speedily crushed by Cromwell's New Model Army. The monarchy was not, in fact, restored in Britain until 1660 with the return of the exiled Charles II from Europe.

Most early historians of the Civil War skirt any mention of atrocities between the opposing forces, and the first important reference to such was to be found in the pages of Sir Walter Scott's novel *Woodstock*, published in 1826, which mentions that 'during the great civil war, 1642-7, the Cavaliers were debited with the atrocity of cannibalism'. The source of this information was said to be an extremely rare pamphlet written during the conflict by one John Lilburne.

To be fair, it has to be stated that Lilburne (c. 1614-57) has been referred to by later historians as a 'notorious demagogue' and his republican agitations had led to him being whipped and imprisoned by the Star Chamber as early as 1638. He found kindred spirits in the Parliamentarian forces, however, and with Cromwell's ascendancy, rose in the army to the rank of lieutenant colonel. Even under the Commonwealth, though, he continued to demand greater reforms, and was repeatedly imprisoned for his treasonable pamphlets which appeared in the years before his death at Eltham.

It was this man, then, who assembled the accusations against the Cavalier, Sir Thomas Lunsford, and some doubt can certainly be cast on the more outlandish of his claims.

The evidence is presented in Lilburne's pamphlet in which he claims of Lunsford, 'his favourite food was the flesh of children', and that he had been witnessed 'like an ogre in the act of cutting a child into steaks and broiling them'. The author also maintained that this 'horrible appetite' was shared by the troops under Lunsford's command who were known as 'The Babe Eaters'. Lilburne asserted that there were witnesses who had seen the Royalist soldiers at their 'unspeakable repast of infants' limbs' and grieving parents who could account for stolen children.

That Lunsford was a man of wild spirits who assembled a reckless and dissolute band of supporters of the King under his banner as 'Sir Thomas Lunsford's Light Horse' seems beyond dispute. His loyalty to the King was also fierce and dedicated, and he had an intense hatred for all those who wished the monarch to be deposed. Indeed, he fought in several of the early skirmishes in 1642 and 1643 and distinguished himself by his mixture of bravery and the savage cut and thrust of his weapons.

The legend of his suspected cannibalism was first prompted by a claim that after one of the earliest encounters he had dismounted from his horse, wiped the blood from the head-wound of a fallen Roundhead, and putting his fingers to his lips declared that he 'hoped to taste the blood of every traitor to His Majesty' before he died.

Within months of this story becoming common gossip, some lines of doggerel were being repeated about Lunsford in almost every Parliamentary household as well as reprinted in broadsheets which attacked the Royalist cause:

'They fear the giblets of his train, they fear
Even his dog, that four-legged cavalier:
He that devours the scraps which Lunsford makes,
Whose picture feeds upon a child in stakes (sic).'

The bizarre story which was to firmly fix the accusation of flesh-eating to Lunsford and his men occurred early in the year 1643 when they were skirmishing with Cromwell's troops at Brentford in Middlesex. Following a brief fight in the High Street with a smaller band of Roundheads who had turned tail and run, one of the soldiers called out to some of the villagers who were cowering behind the windows in their homes, 'Come – have you any fat babies for our breakfast?'

Some subsequent accounts of this incident insist it was no more than a derisory shout from the victorious troops who were well aware of their reputation. Another says the command was taken literally.

'And an old woman brought out a plump baby

boy and proffered him for a meal,' says a copy of this account which has also been quoted in *Notes & Queries*. 'When the trooper hesitated, the woman informed him that the brat was a parish nurse-child and that his board had just been paid for half a year in advance.'

It was Lunsford himself, though, who rode forward and took the child from the old woman, placing the infant on the pommel of his saddle and carrying him away. Lilburne, in his pamphlet, maintains that the Cavalier and his men later dined on this boy; Zachery Gray, a Civil War historian writing in 1716, offered a quite different version. According to him, Sir Thomas gave orders that the boy was to be taken into care and raised at his expense. As the child's name was unknown he was thereafter to be called Cavalier Breakfast!

Although there are only a couple more very unspecific instances of cannibalism charged against Lunsford before his death during the siege of Bristol in 1643 – and whether real or imaginary it has proved impossible to determine – the legend around his name grew the moment he fell. Another doggerel ballad composed as soon as his death was known declared to all who purchased the penny sheet on which it was printed:

'The post that came from Banbury,
Riding in a blue rocket.
He swore he saw when Lunsford fell,
A child's arm in his pocket.'

Such allegations continued to be made against the Royalist troops in succeeding years, as another stanza taken from Thomas Macauley's powerful ballad about 'The Battle of Naseby', which took place in 1645, makes plain:

'Ho! comrades, scour the plain; and ere ye strip the slain,
First give another stab to make your search secure;
Then shake from sleeves and pockets their broad-pieces and lockets,
The tokens of the wanton, the plunder of the poor.'

As Macauley was known to have been a great reader of contemporary ballads and popular rhymes about the Civil War, some experts on the Civil War have seen these lines as further evidence of Royalist troops abusing the bodies of their enemies. One such writer, Jonathan Bouchier, took up the point in an essay, 'Alleged Cannibalism of Soldiers' published in 1888:

'That belief in this propensity to so revolting an indulgence among a certain section of the Royalist soldiery was prevalent after the Restoration seems proved by its appearance on the stage,' Bouchier writes, 'it being alluded to as a recognised habit among the King's warriors during the Civil War in a comedy just closed; and there is also an allusion to it in Butler's Hudibras where the words "runs for 't" are made to rhyme with the last of the line, about children "flying for their lives from Lunsford or 'Bloodybones'". It is certain that Lunsford's Light Horse were nicknamed "The Babe-Eaters" during the Civil War.'

The lines to which Bouchier refers in Samuel Butler's poem read: 'Made children, with your tones, to run for 'it – as bad as Bloodybones or Lunsford.'

Additional evidence against Lunsford that he was 'of so brutal an appetite that he would eat children' is also to be found in the massive tome, *'The History of England: From The Beginning of the Reign of King Charles the First to the Restoration of King Charles the Second*, written by the contemporary historian Laurence Echard (1670-1730), and in an anonymous Collection of Loyal Songs published that same century wherein the following lines appear:

'From Fielding and from Vavasour,
Both ill-affected men;
From Lunsford eke deliver us,
That eateth up children.'

Although to be completely objective, the case against 'Bloodybones' and his men is *probable* rather than *certain*, it does throw some interesting light on the little known facet of the Civil War. And however true or false the tales of cannibalism might have been, they were certainly a most effective propaganda tool used by some of the unscrupulous Parliamentarians 'to raise false alarms and to fill the people full of frightful apprehension', to quote Jonathan Bouchier once again.

Nor does the story quite end there. For following the discussion of the case of Sir Thomas Lunsford in *Notes & Queries*, a reader, George F. Merry, wrote from London on 17 September 1887, referring to the old belief that soldiers ate children:

'How true it is that history repeats itself,' Mr Merry said. 'Just fifty years ago I was serving in the army of Don Carlos of Spain. During the retreat which followed the battle of Chiva, in Valencia, on 15 July 1837, we fell back on the line of the Ebro, and halted for the night of the twentieth in the village of Mosqueruela. Amongst our opponents were some of the Portuguese Legion, serving in Spain under the orders of Baron das Andas; and, being in Carlist country, these gentry took rather freely to helping themselves to food when their regular rations ran short, which, I may observe, not infrequently happened.

'Judge my astonishment on being gravely informed by the good women of Mosqueruela that Portuguese soldiers ate children whenever they found an opportunity of doing so without being observed. "Then you have never seen them do it?" I remarked. "No," was the candid reply I received; but my informant added that one woman only just succeeded in saving her child, which had been tied up during her absence ready to be thrown into a cauldron of soup had her return to the house been longer delayed. This argument was too absurd for me to listen to without a smile, but the women firmly believed what they told me.'

The Witches' Pie

Among the many horrifying practices that have been attributed to witches and warlocks throughout history is that of cannibalism. Indeed, from the evidence of the very earliest records relating to witchcraft, which predate Christianity itself, those who were in league with the Devil were believed to eat human flesh and drink human blood as part of their rituals.

In the first century AD, for instance, Minucius Felix, a Latin scholar, wrote of the contemporary followers of witchcraft, 'As for the initiation of new members, the details are as disgusting as they are well known. A child, covered in dough to deceive the unwary, is set before the would-be novice who is called upon to stab the child to death. Then – it is horrible to see ! – they drink the child's blood and compete with one another as they divide his limbs.'

Turn the clock forward almost two thousand

years and we have Maureen Davies, the director of the Reachout Trust, which has made a special study into modern black magic, with this to say on the same subject: 'Urine and excrement are mixed with blood and semen and the children are made to eat it. Teenage girls and adult women have to sacrifice their own children and after the sacrifice they take out the heart, spleen and eyes and eat them. The children are also taught how to remove parts of the body . . .'

And, as if this were not horrifying enough, Ms Davies reports, 'Some of the bodies are even melted down. The fat is used for candles and the bones ground down and the powder is used as an aphrodisiac.'

Although it is true that the practice of witchcraft and the conducting of black magic rites have been lumped together throughout much of recorded history, in the more enlightened twentieth century we have come to appreciate that there is actually a difference between the two. Witchcraft, or to be precise *Wicca*, is an ancient fertility religion several thousand years old that worships the ancient gods of nature; while black magic is a convenient cover for allowing free reign to the evil side of man's nature in perverted nocturnal orgies of indiscriminate sex and violence.

It is also true to say that over the centuries the public's view of witches formed into a classic stereotype – an aged hag who apparently had the power to fly on a broomstick and, in return for obedience to the Evil One, was enabled to work magic on man or beast. In fact, practitioners could be men as well as women; the only 'flying' they did was when they were high on special ointments inhaled or rubbed on their bodies and made from a mixture of plants such as hemlock and belladonna, the crushed bodies of venomous reptiles, small animals, roots and metals; and their magic was more often than not simple deception working on superstitious fears.

Many an unfortunate old man or woman who was going senile was deemed to be a witch by neighbours who took their harmless muttering as prayers to the Devil and the squinting of their rheumy eyes as attempts to put the 'Evil Eye' upon some innocent man, woman or child. If the old soul happened to possess a household pet such as a cat or dog, even a chicken, duck, rabbit or mouse, this was deemed to be their 'familiar spirit' and final proof of a pact with the Evil One.

John Gaule, an Essex clergyman writing in 1646, summed up the public's mania about witches in these words: 'Every old woman with a wrinkled face, a furr'd brow, a hairy lip, a gobber tooth, a squint eye, having a ragged coat on her back, a skull cap on her head, a dog or cat by her side, is not only suspected, but pronounced for a witch.'

Followers of witchcraft were also believed to hold special meetings, or Sabbats, at which the Devil – represented by one of their number – was worshipped and a banquet held in his honour.

These feasts did not consist of any ordinary meal, but were an orgy of gluttony and lust as a certain Sister Madeleine de Demandolx revealed in 1611:

'The drink which they have is malmsey to provoke and prepare the flesh to luxurious wantonness,' the Sister said. 'The meat they ordinarily eat is the flesh of young children, which they cook and make ready beforehand, sometimes bringing the children thither alive by stealing them from houses where they have an opportunity to go unseen. They have no use of knives at table for fear lest they should be laid in the sign of the cross. They have also no salt, which figureth out wisdom and understanding; neither know they the use of olives or oil which represent mercy.'

A group of witches in Berne confessed that they cooked babies in a cauldron, 'until the whole flesh comes away from the bones to make a soup which may easily be drunk'; while in Spain it was said to be a common practice for live animals to be torn limb from limb and then eaten at the 'feasts'.

That such events also took place in England at this time is attested to in the trial of a notorious group of Lancashire witches that was held in 1612. One of the chief defendants, a woman known as Old Chattox, told the court of her family's meeting with that of another witch at the Malking Tower.

'There was victuals in plenty', she said, 'including flesh, butter, cheese, bread and drink. And after their eating, the devil called Fancy and the other spirit calling himself Tibbe carried the remnants away. And although we did eat, we were never the fuller nor the better for it.'

Among the many people who were accused of being in league with the Devil at this time, a great many were undoubtedly innocent. But there were certainly others who *did* seek the dark path and were prepared to pay almost any price in return for what they believed would be supernatural powers.

One such person was Mary Johnson, a young woman in her twenties who lived on her own in a tiny cottage in Wivenhoe, Essex. In 1645 she was said to have poisoned two children in order to cannibalise their bodies. Mary wanted the flesh to make one of the infamous 'Witches' Pies', a portion of which, it was believed, would prevent anyone who ate it from confessing to witchcraft. This 'confession' was a prequisite of the law at the time to enforce the death penalty.

Essex, where Mary lived, has gone down in history as the 'Witch County' – a sobriquet which is not difficult to understand when appreciating the fact that during the 150 years from 1559, the number of indictments for witchcraft in the county – 473 – was larger than the total for the four other counties in the Judicial Home Circuit: Kent, Surrey, Sussex and Hertfordshire, which had a grand total of 317. Among those charged, many were victimised old crones, both men and women, but Mary's case stands apart from the rest as being one of the few with the evidence of actual bodies against her. What she was apparently seeking from her gruesome act has been graphically explained by Margaret Murray, a leading expect on witchcraft, in her essay, 'Child Sacrifices Among European Witches', published in 1918.

'The sacrifice of a child was usually performed as a means of procuring certain magical materials or powers,' she wrote, 'which were obtained by preparing the sacrificed bodies in several ways. Reginald Scot in his *Discovery of Witchcraft* (1584) says that the flesh of the child was boiled and consumed by the witches for two purposes. Of the thicker part of the concoction, "they make ointments whereby they ride in the air; but the thinner portion they put into flaggons whereof whosoever drinketh, observing certain ceremonies, immediately becomes a master or mistress in that practice and facility".'

Margaret Murray goes on, 'A gang of Paris witches confessed that they "distilled" the entrails of a sacrificed child after celebrating a mass for Madame de Montespan, the method being probably that described by Scot. At Forfar in 1661, Helen Guthrie and four others also exhumed the body of an unbaptised infant which was buried in the churchyard near the south-east door of the church "to make a pie thereof that they might eat of it and by this means might never make a confession (as they thought) of their witchcrafts". For it was believed that witches could not be condemned and burned without having first confessed.'

It was a pie very much like this one that Mary Johnson prepared from the bodies of the two children she lured into her tiny home and poisoned.

Wivenhoe, where she lived, was an isolated little village on the River Colne, just a few miles from Colchester, the famous Roman settlement of Camulodunum, Britain's oldest recorded town. It was a village steeped in superstition where those who pointed the finger accusing of witchcraft at a neighbour were very likely to be believed. That Mary thought she could escape notice says a great deal for the power she attributed to her cannibal pie.

The recipe she used is to be found in another ancient treatise on witchcraft, *Compendium Maleficarum*, assembled from a number of European sources by a seventeenth-century Italian scholar, Francesco-Maria Guazzo.

Having obtained the body, says the recipe, 'the witches take several pieces thereof, as the feet, hands, a part of the head, and a part of the buttock, and cook this in a sauce made of blood and malmsy'. The resulting stew could be eaten either on its own or with a crust of pastry made from holy wafers stolen from a church, stated Guazzo.

The records of Mary's arrest indicate that it was the stench caused by the remains of the two bodies which she kept in her house that first alerted her neighbours to what had occurred. And when she was seized by the local magistrate, Mary apparently still had a portion of the pie in a bowl in her kitchen. It seems she made no attempt to conceal the contents of the pie, believing, presumably, in its power to prevent her from confessing to witchcraft.

At Mary's subsequent trial at Chelmsford in April 1645 she was charged with poisoning the two children – 'all the symptoms suggest strychnine' according to Margaret Murray who studied the case history – and, having been found guilty, she was ordered to be executed. Curiously, there was only a passing mention of the Witches' Pie during the proceedings and it played no part in her conviction. In that fact alone, it might be said to have carried out its purpose in sparing her from being hanged with the label of 'witch' around her head.

The association of Devil-worship and cannibalism has continued in succeeding centuries. Indeed as recently as 1991 flesh-eating was said to have taken place during what became known as the 'Satanic Child Abuse Case' which also occurred in Essex. These events, which were stated to have taken place in Epping Forest, involved sacrificial rituals, sex orgies and eating the bodies of infants.

According to the evidence which was given in court when the case came to trial in November 1991, a coven of Satanists had been in the habit of meeting in the forest and placing new-born babies on an altar and ritually killing them. Young girls who were present were alleged to have been forced to dismember the corpses and eat the flesh. On some occasions they were also made to drink the still warm blood.

At least three babies and three young children were claimed to have died, and similar rituals were said to have taken place in the living-rooms of some of the members' homes in nearby South Woodford. The bodies were then either buried in the forest or stowed away in plastic bags until they could be burned. Allegations of animal slaughter, sexual abuse of the young girls by male cultists and orgies at which aphrodisiac drinks were served, were also presented by the Crown prosecution during the week-long trial at the Old Bailey.

At the end of five days, however, the trial collapsed when the prosecution counsel admitted he had serious doubts about the truth of the confessions from the two young girls who appeared in the witness box as the main witnesses to the abuse and cannibalism. The accused three men and two women were set free and there can be little doubt that justice was done. But the case highlighted once again the fact that even now as we approach the dawn of the twenty-first century, the ancient fears of witchcraft and Devil-worship have still not disappeared.

The Flesh Shops of Brazil

Of all the races of the world who have practised cannibalism, the Brazilians are said to have made the business of preparing and cooking human flesh into almost an art form. Records in the nation's archives indicate that in earlier years practitioners not only devised a number of recipes for the serving of flesh, but even ran 'butcher shops at which the choicest cuts of human flesh were served.'

To be sure, such practices were in the main to be found in the villages of the interior of the country rather than in the towns along the more civilised east coast. But there is no denying how widespread the habit was, as can be seen from studying various reports compiled by travellers of the time. A typical account is to be found in G H Von Langsdorff's *Voyages and Travels in Various Parts of the World*, published in 1795.

'Incredible as it may appear,' Langsdorff wrote,

'there have been, and still are, particularly in South America, especially in the interior of Brazil, people who feed upon human flesh merely on account of its delicacy, and as the height of gourmandise. These people not only eat the prisoners they take in battle, but sometimes even their own kin; they also buy and sell human flesh publicly. To them we are indebted for the information that white men are finer-flavoured than negroes, and that Englishmen are preferable to Frenchmen. Further, the flesh of young girls and women, particularly of new-born children, far exceeds in delicacy that of the finest youths or grown men. Finally, they tell us that the inside of the hand and the sole of the foot are the nicest parts of the human body.'

Another visitor to Brazil in the sixteenth century, Michel de Montaigne, wrote an entire essay, 'On Cannibals', in which he said that ritual cannibalism was deeply entrenched in the nation's psyche. 'A merchant who had lived there for some years told me that everyone for a trophy brings home the head of an enemy he has killed and eaten which he then fixes over the door of his house.'

According to this same source, the Brazilians would also keep alive a number of prisoners, cosset them to ensure they were happy, and deliberately fatten them up. 'Then they invite along a great assembly of friends and, having tidily despatched one of the prisoners, they roast him, eat him amongst them, and send some chops to their absent friends,' says Montaigne.

Robert Southey in his *History of Brazil* (1810) goes into even greater detail about one of these grisly cannibal feasts:

'At all the flesh-eating operations, old women presided, and they derived so much importance from these occasions that their exultation over a prisoner was fiend-like. They stood by the fire and caught the fat as it fell, that nothing might be lost, licking their fingers during their accursed employment.

'Every part of the body was devoured; the arm and thigh bones were reserved to be made into flutes; the teeth strung in necklaces; and the skull was set up at the entrance of the town, or it was sometimes used as a drinking cup, after the manner of our Scandinavian ancestors. The Brazilians have learned to consider human flesh as the most exquisite of all dainties. Delicious, however, as these repasts were deemed, they derived their highest flavour from revenge.'

At the centre of the trade in human flesh in Brazil at this time was said to be a family named Floreal whose 'shop' was located in the heart of the Matto Grosso at a town appropriately named Mortes. An anonymous engraving from the sixteenth century shows a group of people believed to be the Floreals and their assistants, male and female, young and old, all preparing some 'choice cuts.'

In the archives of the Matto Grosso region now

housed in Brasilia are a number of the recipes which a certain Joao Floreal is said to have learned from his forebears and committed to paper during the later part of the seventeenth century.

Pride of place in the collection goes to smoked meat, which is said to have been one of the most popular forms of preparing human flesh in the country for centuries. The cuts were first salted, Floreal wrote, then smoked over an open fire and kept until required. The best smoked meat was deemed to be made from the thighs, the ribs and a fleshy backside. The liver, heart and brains were also considered to make ideal titbits.

Stew was apparently also high among the favourites of the Brazilian cannibals. To make this, the flesh had to be cut into pieces 'the size of a man's fist' and boiled in not too much water with a seasoning of salt and peppers. The pot had to be simmered from mid-morning to late in the after-noon, when it would be ready for serving at the evening meal with vegetables and fruit.

Roasted human flesh had to be prepared rather differently, however. Firstly, the meat had to be cut into chunks, 'none larger than the leg of a sheep.' After this the flesh required washing and sprinkling with salt before being fixed on iron spikes over wood embers.

The cuts had to be roasted very gently and turned regularly, according to Joao Floreal, as well as being basted from time to time with fresh oil. To make for the best eating, the cuts were roasted from late at night until early in the morning, when they were ready for serving with potatoes and other vegetables.

Reading the recipes in Floreal's collection it is very easy to forget that he is talking about human flesh. And his descriptions of dismembering a corpse are so matter-of-fact as to make the reader almost believe he is referring to butchering an animal such as a sheep or cow.

The same cannot be said for an anonymous account of a meal of human flesh which, according to the document on which it is written, was prepared not so many years ago at Penedo, a town on the east coast of Brazil between Recife and Salvador. The body was that of a teenage girl who had been sacrificed at one of the country's infamous voodoo rites. The child had allegedly been ceremonially strangled by a 'papaloi' – one of the cult's priests – and then prepared for eating. I have edited out some of the more unpleasant elements from the account of what happened next:

'The priest then handed the cannibal chef a large knife with which he cut the girl's head off, his assistants catching her blood in a jar. After flaying the body with a leather thong, the flesh was cut from the bones and placed in large wooden dishes. The entrails and skin were taken outside and buried.

'Now the chef began to prepare his feast in earnest, cooking the flesh with some small and rather bitter beans and a number of yams. While this was going on, he also cut a piece of flesh from one of the child's palms which lay on a dish and ate it raw with every sign of enjoyment.

'At last when the flesh was cooked, everyone sat down and partook of the meal, drinking the soup which had been made during the cooking and collected into earthenware pots. There followed much dancing, drinking and debauchery, and in the morning the remains of the flesh were heated up and served to the revellers before they returned to their homes.'

Accounts of cannibalism being practised as part of voodoo have also been reported this century from Haiti, the island sandwiched between South America and the United States. Here the sacrifice of animals and chickens is an almost everyday occurrence, and human blood is also occasionally spilled to propitiate the gods of voodoo.

But sometimes it can be more than just blood which is spilt. According to a report by-lined Port-au-Prince and carried in the *Miami Herald* only five years ago, 'Although a white cock or a white kid is the usual victim of a voodoo sacrifice, there have undoubtedly been occasions when a 'goat-without-horns' has been used. To those not familiar with this euphemism it means 'girl child'."

The Edinburgh Body-Snatcher

Among its many claims to fame, the historic Scottish city of Edinburgh is still known as the home of the body-snatchers, the infamous men (and a few women, too) who stole dead bodies from graveyards in order to sell them to surgeons and their students so that they might 'further the cause of medical science'.

The city's reputation is, in the main, built on the activities of two men: William Burke and William Hare, who were not content with grave-robbing, but in nine hectic months butchered sixteen people and sold their corpses to satisfy what was then a huge local demand for bodies for dissection. Although Burke was arrested and hanged in 1829, Hare turned King's evidence and, set free, was last seek 'walking towards England'. Behind him, though, he and his partner left a legend that has survived to this day.

But Burke and Hare were actually just two of the

hordes of cannibals in both Scotland and England who went out in search of 'things for the surgeons' and made the expression that a person was 'worth more dead than alive' literally true. For years, a large percentage of the population of the British Isles went in fear of what might happen to their bodies after they were dead – for such was the demand for bodies at the great medical schools and hospitals that rich and poor alike were equally in danger of ending up under the knife on an operating table or in an anatomy theatre.

The only bodies that were officially available for dissection during the later half of the eighteenth century were those of people who had been hanged for murder. Unofficially, though, the authorities had for years turned a blind eye to the trade of the resurrectionists, allowing the medical fraternity to make their own deals with the 'burkers' or 'sack-em-up men', as these ghoulish grave-robbers were popularly known.

Those men and women who had died as paupers were undoubtedly the most vulnerable to the attentions of the body-snatchers, since they were usually buried in shallow graves and sometimes two or three to a plot. All the resurrectionists needed to do was to take a quiet Sunday afternoon stroll – for this was the day on which most working class people were buried – and, having spotted a new internment, return in the evening to bribe the watchman and then quickly dig up their victim. It was said that skilled body-snatchers could remove a body, and replace the grave so that it looked as if it had never been touched, in under ninety minutes.

According to most accounts of this nefarious trade, if the robbers were seen in the street with a corpse by anyone but relatives of the dead person, they were unlikely to be challenged. Indeed, it is said that purloined bodies often literally became a favourite cover for other items of stolen property.

The corpses were invariably taken in at night by the surgeons and schools and never a question was asked about their origins. Dr Robert Knox, the Edinburgh anatomist who was ruined because of his dealings with Burke and Hare, was said to have paid out about £800 in one year to keep his students supplied with bodies for dissection. And another Edinburgh man, the surgeon Robert Liston, was even reputed to have gone out hunting for bodies himself with the 'burkers', and took part in a number of raids on cemeteries in the fishing villages of Fife just across the Firth of Forth.

The demand for bodies was always heaviest in the winter months when both the doctors and students were at their busiest, and some of the less scrupulous medical men even paid their regular body-snatchers a retainer's fee! And if one of the resurrectionists was unlucky enough to be caught and imprisoned, the man he supplied had to help maintain the corpse-thief's wife and family – or else there was a very real danger the prisoner would inform on the doctor who had used his services and get him jailed too.

A well-known trick employed by some of the most villainous body-snatchers involved delivering the corpse to a dissecting room, collecting the fee, and then returning later in the dead of night to steal it again and sell it on to another customer. Some Scottish 'burkers' even made a practice of calling on anatomy rooms and claiming that a body which they knew had been deposited there was that of a relative. Then it would be whisked off somewhere else and sold for a second time!

However, in Edinburgh it was not just Burke and Hare who helped give the city such a bad name in the history of body-snatching. For there were others equally unscrupulous who, when the numbers of graves that could be robbed declined (because of greater precautions and more conscientious watchmen), turned instead to murder. They would foray into the backstreets of the city with a chloroform pad and a sack to pounce on unsuspecting passersby, especially young women, who would then be summarily killed.

According to historian William Buchanan writing about this 'foulest trade in human history', the body-snatchers of Edinburgh did not just sell the corpses, but would also steal their jewellery, teeth 'and even the fat from their bodies which had a market'. Among their number was a man named Nichol Brown who went further than all the rest by practising cannibalism as well.

Brown was born in what is now the Old Town, somewhere in the vicinity of Candlemarket Row, in the year 1725. Nothing is known of his parents beyond the fact that he was orphaned while still a child and literally grew up in the back alleys, supporting himself by thieving. About 1745 he joined a gang of 'sack-em-up men' who preyed on cemeteries in the city.

Nichol Brown was a big, strapping man who used his brawn in helping his associates to empty graves as quickly as any of their brotherhood. On an average night, the four men of the group expected to be able to exhume the same number of corpses and deliver them to their customers before dawn broke. The evidence suggests that Brown's enthusiasm for the dead bodies which they dug up soon went further than mere commercial ends. In fact, he began expressing a desire to taste the flesh of their victims.

When Brown was later brought to trial it was stated that he so upset his companions with these ideas that they told him they would only go along with him when they were unable to manage without his great strength. Unperturbed, he insisted upon being allowed to cut off some of the flesh from at least one of the bodies they dug up, preferably that of a young female.

Although Nichol Brown undoubtedly revolted his fellow robbers, his complete lack of squeamishness is said to have made him useful to at least one Edinburgh surgeon who occasionally employed him as an assistant on his experiments. Brown may well have been a vulgar and unpleasant man, but the facts suggest that he also had an instinctive grasp of anatomy which made him useful to the surgeon. And as part-payment for his assistance, it is believed that Brown was allowed to take away the hearts and livers of some of the bodies which the pair dissected.

Brown then took these titbits home to his wife, a downtrodden and unhappy woman he had married in 1750. She was forced to cook them for their meals, though whether she knew they were human remains is unknown. But as the poor woman knew her husband's occupation – he often boasted to her of the number of graves he had robbed in an evening – the suspicion remains that she must have had a pretty good idea.

Nichol Brown certainly earned good money from this 'burking', though he also spent lavishly and enjoyed nothing more than a drunken spree with his cronies. During one of these at his favourite inn in Leith, he boasted to the assembled company about his appetite for human flesh.

'The flesh o' some young bairn tastes better than yon lamb or beef.' he growled into his mug. 'Aye, 'een that of a poor muckle man is better.'

For a moment laughter rolled around the dark and smoky interior of the inn, until the other men realised Brown was being serious.

'Away with ye,' one slightly braver than the rest replied. 'How would ye know? Ye'll ha' to prove it.'

At this, Brown stood up and banged his mug on

the table. Certainly he would prove it to them, he said, he would bring a piece of human flesh to the inn and roast and eat it before their very eyes. And where would Brown get this meat? Why, from the body of a criminal who had just been hanged.

The inn fell silent. Everyone knew about the man's activities as a grave-robber. But would he go so far as to steal the flesh from the body of a gibbeted man?

The next evening the men got their answer when Brown strode into the bar with a portion of a dead man's leg in a small sack under his arm. He had taken it, he said, from the body of Norman Ross, a criminal hanged a week earlier, whose corpse had been left hanging as a deterrent. He had used his knowledge of anatomy to slip up to the gibbet under cover of darkness and slice off part of Ross's leg. The men looked at each other and shuddered.

There was total silence as Brown removed the grisly joint from his sack and tied it on to a spit over the fire. There he sat in silence for an hour while the flames turned the piece of leg pink and then greyish-brown. When he finally put the roasted flesh to his lips, even the most hardened customer in the inn lost interest in his ale.

The legend of Nichol Brown's cannibal feast soon became common tavern gossip around Edinburgh, but it was not this act which would earn him his lasting notoriety. That began when he added murder to his list of crimes by killing his wife in August 1754.

Right from the start of their marriage, Brown had proved himself a cruel and heartless husband. He frequently beat his wife and was especially vicious after nights of drinking. The slightest word of protest would be answered by a hail of blows and kicks.

One night early in that month of August he returned home even more drunk than usual. His poor wife was huddled over a tiny fire attempting to cook herself a small piece of meat. Seeing what she was doing, Brown snatched the morsel from her and jammed it into his mouth. It was barely cooked, and the drunken man spat it out with a violent oath.

Seizing his wife by the hair, Brown then proceeded to beat her about the head until she collapsed, a bleeding and already dying figure, on to the stone floor. As Brown himself slumped down by the fireside, she gave a final small cry and died.

Some time later, Brown became aware of what he had done. He looked at the figure on the floor and knew he could hang for his crime. In his fuddled state he realised he must get rid of the body. But how?

His solution – as the subsequent trial was to hear – was horrifyingly simple. Nichol Brown decided to dismember the corpse of his wife, roast her flesh and eat her. Although those who attended the trial were spared the full details of this monstrous act, the prosecution stated that Brown not only swallowed nearly all the evidence of this crime, but also hid the remaining bones by burying them nearby, close to Edinburgh Castle.

When Brown's wife was missed by her neighbours, he attempted to explain this away by saying that she had gone away to visit some relatives in Berwick. But it was his vanity that would give him away. Once again, when in his cups at the inn in Leith, he could not resist an even more monstrous boast. He had killed and eaten his wife, he told his cronies, and how could anyone prove it because there was no body?

On this occasion, however, Nichol Brown's self-assurance was misplaced. His wild story eventually came to the ears of the authorities, and bluster as he might that without a corpse he could not be tried, the former body-snatcher was hauled into court and there the grisly details of his crime were revealed. The smirk which had sat on his face throughout the proceedings was wiped away when the judge sentenced him to be hanged in chains.

There was to be one more grim episode in the life of the Edinburgh cannibal which would ensure his legend in a most apposite way.

The horrific details of Brown's crimes had made him an object of curiosity to a great many people in Edinburgh, and hundreds trooped out to see him executed and later to gaze at his corpse swinging from the gibbet. But just a week later his body was mysteriously cut down from the gibbet one night and disappeared.

Enquiries soon revealed, however, that the theft had been perpetrated by some medical students from the university who had been appalled at the tales of Nichol Brown's cannibalism and tossed his corpse into a nearby pond. The pond was dragged and soon the body was back on the gibbet once more.

Then, two nights later, it went missing again. This time it was no students' prank, and even a substantial reward offered for the return of the malefactor's remains produced nothing. Indeed, the mystery of precisely *what* happened to Brown's body has remained from that day to this.

But there is, nevertheless, a persistent rumour that the former resurrectionist got his just deserts in the end. That his corpse was stolen secretly by some body-snatchers and ended up like all those which he himself had handled – under an Edinburgh surgeon's knife . . .

The Demon Barber of Paris

Adjoining the Pont St Michel which links Paris to the Île de la Cité on the River Seine is the ancient, dog-leg street of the rue de la Harpe. It stands within sight of the impressive Palais de Justice and the Gothic splendour of the Cathedral of Notre Dame – both favourite spots with the millions of tourists who visit the city each year.

The law courts are, of course, very much associated with the legendary policemen of the city like George Simenon's Maigret; while Notre Dame is forever mentioned in the same breath as the classic novel by Victor Hugo about the tormented Hunchback of Notre Dame, which has been filmed several times. Yet the rue de la Harpe is also the focal point of a tale of crime and horror about a barber who, in the closing years of the eighteenth century, murdered his clients and with an associate had their corpses turned into meat pies. Some historians have even suggested these events were the inspiration for that famous London story of Sweeney Todd, the Demon Barber of Fleet Street . . .

Rue de la Harpe, in the faubourg St Marcel, runs from the busy Boulevard Saint Germain to the Place Marcel beside the Seine. Today it is a hive of modern shops and offices, but at the time of the demon barber it was 'a long, dismal ancient street', according to an account of the bloodthirsty crimes written by Joseph Fouche in a volume entitled *Archives of the Police*, published in 1816.

Fouche's version of the events states that at the time of his writing, the shop in the rue de la Harpe where the customers were murdered for their money had already been razed to the ground because of public horror at what had occurred within its walls. He writes, 'There is a space or gap in the line of buildings upon which formerly stood two dwelling houses now marked by a melancholy memorial signifying that upon this spot no human habitation shall ever be erected and no human being must ever reside! Curiosity will of course be greatly excited to ascertain what it was that rendered this devoted spot so obnoxious to humanity, and yet so interesting to history.'

Any visitor to Paris who goes to the rue de la Harpe in the hope of finding any trace of this 'obnoxious spot' will be disappointed; but the legend of the barber, whose name is believed to have been Becque, and his infamous associate the pie-maker, lives on.

The shop which the barber – or perruquier, as

they were known at the time – owned and ran was apparently an unprepossessing, rather squalid little building, a short distance down the rue de la Harpe from the Place St Michel. Behind the grimy windows, a number of wigs were set on false heads, while in the shop itself all the furnishings were rudimentary. A shaving chair for the customers was situated in the centre of the room, while on the wall beside a small stove which served to heat the water for shaves was an array of razors, combs and scissors: the tools of the barber's trade.

Next door to the perruquier's premises stood the shop of a pastry-cook. This was apparently a much more attractive-looking building, with its door usually wide open to allow the smells of fresh baking to filter into the street and tempt the appetites of passing Parisians. According to the legend, the shop was 'so remarkable for savoury patties that these were sent for to the rue de la Harpe from the most distant parts of Paris'.

To all intents and purposes, though, these two shops were like many other small businesses to be found in the side-streets of the capital at the end of the eighteenth century. The events which were to bring the hideous truth to light about what had been happening between the two shopkeepers working in collusion were to begin in a most prosaic way.

One morning in the spring of 1800, two travellers were making their way up the rue de la Harpe from the rue St Germain to a business meeting in the Notre Dame quarter. The pair were friends and neighbours, both wealthy men, who lived on the outskirts of the city. They planned to carry out certain money transactions and then return to their homes as soon as possible.

'They were on foot,' says the account by Joseph Fouche, 'a very common way even at present, for persons of much respectability, to travel in France, and were attended, as most pedestrians are, by a faithful dog.

'Upon their arrival at the rue de la Harpe, they stepped into the shop of a perruquier to be shaved, before they would proceed to business or enter into the more fashionable streets. So limited was their time, and peremptory was their return, that the first man who was shaved proposed to his companion that while he was undergoing the operation of the razor, he who was already shaven would run and execute a small commission in the neighbourhood, promising that he would be back before the other was ready to move. For this purpose he left the shop of the barber.'

Nothing untoward so far. But when the traveller returned to the shop a little while later, he was informed by the barber that his companion had already left. Somewhat puzzled, he presumed his friend had only gone for a few moments to somewhere close by and would soon be back. His conviction was rather confirmed by the fact that the other man's dog was still sitting patiently outside the front door. He, too, sat down on a small bench.

But an hour passed and there was still no sign of his friend. The dog also remained lying outside the door, showing no sign of wanting to move.

'Did he leave no message?' the traveller finally asked the barber who had been continuing with his work refurbishing a wig.

'No, sir,' the man said without looking up. 'He was shaved and went away. It was certainly very odd.'

Another hour passed and still there was no sign of the missing traveller. By now, though, the dog was beginning to show the same signs of unease as the man.

'The poor animal exhibited marks of restlessness in yelps and in howlings,' Fouche's report continues, 'which so affected the sensibilities of the traveller that he threw out some insinuations not much to the credit of the barber, who indignantly ordered him to quit his boutique. Upon quitting the shop, he found it impossible to remove the dog from the door. No whistling, no calling, no patting would do, stir he would not.

'In his agony, the afflicted man raised a crowd about the door, to whom he told his lamentable story. The dog became an object of universal interest and of close attention. He shivered and he howled, but no seduction, no caressing, no experiment, could make him desert his post.'

As the crowd around the perruquier's grew larger and the mystery concerning the traveller's inexplicable disappearance was passed from mouth to mouth, it was suggested by one passerby that the police should be called. Another voice was raised to demand that an immediate search of the premises should be made, as it seemed increasingly likely from the animal's devoted behaviour that his master had never left the shop.

Finally, the remaining traveller and several members of the crowd forced their way past the protesting barber and into his shop. Every room in the small building was searched, but no trace of the other man could be found. A rather curious small pile of hats and cloaks discovered in an upstairs room was quickly dismissed as lost property . . .

'After a fruitless search and much altercation,' says Fouche, 'the barber, who had prevailed upon those who had forced into his house, to quit, came to the door and, haranguing the populace, declared most solemnly his innocence. Suddenly the dog, which had remained sentinel at the shop door all this time, sprang upon the barber and flew at his throat in a state of terrific exasperation. At this, his victim fainted and was with the utmost difficulty rescued from being torn to pieces. The dog seemed to be in a state of intellectual agony and fury.'

Seeing the barber lying unconscious, the friend of the missing traveller now had an another idea. He suggested that the animal should be allowed into the shop to see if it could find anything. The instant the door was thrown open the dog did not need a second invitation to go inside.

Sniffing furiously around the shaving room, the creature seemed to pick up a scent and darted down some stairs which the earlier searchers had obviously missed. The dog could soon be heard howling in what must be an underground cellar. So dark was the place, though, that none of the searchers could see anything, and a call was made for find some lamps.

The scene which greeted the traveller and the other handful of passersby who squeezed into the cellar was to remain with them for the rest of their lives. In the light of a flickering oil lamp they made out dank walls splattered with blood, and on a table in the middle of the cellar, a headless torso from which the limbs had been severed. These arms and legs bore every sign that the flesh had been stripped away from them.

Beneath the table with its grisly burden lay several items of clothing which the traveller at once recognised as having belonged to his friend. In the midst of these were two disembodied hands which the dog was now licking plaintively.

For some minutes the little party stood dumb with horror. Not only had the missing man quite clearly been murdered, but his body was now apparently in the process of being butchered like a piece of meat. But *why*?

The tears of sorrow which had welled up in the traveller's eyes at this discovery were now replaced with a sense of anger and outrage. To kill a man for his money was one thing, but to treat his body in this manner was obscene, almost unbelievable.

Slowly the man raised his eyes from the bloody carnage on the table. And as he did so, he caught sight of a half-open hatchway at the far end of the cellar. It looked as if it had been in use recently; might even have been about to be used again when whoever was using the cellar was disturbed. He moved across the room and thrust the lamp through the hatch.

Even before the light illuminated what was beyond the hatch, a smell assailed his nostrils. A smell he remembered from earlier in the day. The smell of baking savoury patties.

Shock and disbelief now crossed his face. The hatch was clearly linked to the baker's shop next-door to the barber's. The perruquier and the pie-maker were clearly partners in some terrible trade. And when the traveller called the others to see what he had discovered, their eyes met in mutual admission of what they hardly dared imagine.

There was the evidence that the barber had been removing the flesh from his victims to provide meat for the pastry-cook. In this ingenious way, all the evidence of the men's crime could be removed. Doubtless both shared in the proceeds.

But what they saw also prompted an even more gruesome conclusion. There was undoubtedly a highly organised system in operation here. How many times had it been used before?

The barber was by now recovering consciousness in his shop, and as soon as the traveller returned from the cellar he ordered that the police be called. He was anxious that no one else should enter the dungeon of horrors for fear that the public's anger would quickly turn to revulsion and then a demand for revenge before the law could take its course.

By the time the officers from the nearby Prefecture of Police arrived, the evidence in both shops was plain to see. A tray containing what was obviously human flesh was found in the pastrycook's kitchen – dusted with flour and ready to be made into meat pies – providing the final evidence, if such was needed, of the infamous trade the two men had been carrying out.

Despite their protestations of innocence, Becque and his accomplice, who was later named as Mornay, were hurried swiftly away to cells on the Île de la Cité. By nightfall, news of their terrible activities had spread across Paris and a crowd demanding their blood was besieging the police headquarters. Extra men were needed then to hold back the crowds – as they were at the subsequent trial in the Palais de Justice.

Reporting on this, Joseph Fouche summarises: 'The facts that appeared at their trial and upon confession were these. Those incautious travellers who whilst in the shop of the barber-fiend unhappily talked of the money they had upon them, were, as soon as they had turned their backs, set upon by the wretch. He, who was a robber and murderer by profession, drew his razor across their throats and plundered them of their money.

'Then the pastry-cook whose shop was so remarkable for its savoury patties took possession of the bodies. And those who were murdered by the razor of one were concealed by the knife of the other in those very identical patties, by which, independently of his partnership in those frequent robberies, he had made a fortune.'

Although it proved impossible to put an accurate estimate on the number of victims the two men had killed and turned into meat pies, the evidence of the items of clothing and expensive valuables in the upstairs room of the barber's shop, which had at first been overlooked, pointed to a total of several dozen, perhaps even as many as one hundred. Suffice it to say, the two men were found guilty of mass murder and ordered to be executed.

Fouche also adds an interesting piece of information about the outcome of the events in the rue de la Harpe.

'This case was of so terrific a nature,' he says, 'that it was made part of the sentence of the law, that besides the execution of the monsters, the houses in which they perpetrated those infernal deeds should be pulled down, and that the spot on which they stood should be marked out to posterity with horror and execration.'

Though all traces of the Demon Barber of Paris

have long since disappeared from the neighbourhood of St Marcel, some historians have suggested that the legend provided the basis of the famous tale of London's serial-killer, Sweeney Todd. The location of the killings and pie-making, it would seem, were moved across the Channel to Fleet Street by an ingenious English writer of Penny Dreadfuls named Thomas Peckett Prest, whose serial story 'The String of Pearls', in which Todd first appeared, was published in 1846. Interesting though this theory is, the facts are otherwise, as those who care to read my book, *Sweeney Todd, The Real Story of the Demon Barber of Fleet Street* (also published by Boxtree, 1993) will discover.

Yet the fiend of St Marcel still warrants recognition as one of France's most terrible mass-killers. And if he himself was not actually a cannibal and flesh-eater, those unhappy customers of his partner, Mornay – albeit unknowingly – most certainly were.

The Loathsome Appetite of Antoine Langulet

The famous Paris Opera House has become even more familiar to the general public in recent years as a result of Andrew Lloyd Webber's musical extravaganza, The Phantom of the Opera, based on the classic, though rather neglected, novel of the same title by Gaston Leroux which was first published in 1911. The story of the disfigured musician who haunts the Opera House endeavouring to promote the career of his beautiful young protégée through a mixture of inspiration and fear is widely believed to be a piece of fiction – although, in fact, Leroux based the story on a long-standing tradition that France's first home of opera was haunted by the ghost of a tormented musician.

The architectural magnificence of the Opera House building and the sumptuous decoration of its auditorium have led to it being used as the setting for many of the world's most prestigious operas and ballets. The building itself was not opened until 1875, although the idea for a new opera house in the centre of Paris had been proposed as early as 1820. There, on a site previously occupied by a huddle of ancient slums, the young architect Charles Garnier – who was chosen from a contest of 171 entrants to design the new building – created what is the biggest theatre in the world (with a stage so large it can accommodate 450 actors and actresses) and arguably the most successful monument of the Second Empire.

While the weird story of the ghost that haunts the Opera House may have inspired first a French novelist and then an English composer, there is also a much more horrifying though little-known tale associated with the same area. It, too, occurred in the nineteenth century, although it pre-dates the actual construction of the Opera by half a century. This is the story of the Loathsome Appetite of Antoine Langulet, who is also known as 'The Man-Eater of Clichy'.

Antoine Langulet was an urban cannibal. A man who unashamedly fed on human flesh and of whom it was later written, 'Instances of extraordinary and depraved appetites may be found in the writings of both ancient and modern authors; and there are also many cases on record in which it will be seen that this horrible disease has reached to a most astonishing height. But none of them can parallel the disgusting narrative of Antoine Langulet.'

The Loathsome Appetite of Antoine Langulet

The main source of information about this Parisian flesh-eater is the records of a Dr Berthollet, written in 1825 and preserved in the Archives of the Bicetre Prison in which Langulet ended his days in the middle years of the nineteenth century. Langulet was apparently a bastard child abandoned to the streets of Paris in the early years of the century. He lived in a hovel – in some accounts it was a hayloft – on what is now the avenue de l'Opera, where hs nauseating appetites were first observed by some of the other slum dwellers when he was still a child.

'He had since his youth been in the habit of satisfying an unnatural appetite with food of the most repulsive and disgusting description,' Dr Berthollet wrote in his record of the case. 'It appeared that animal substances in the highest state of putrefaction and even the human body itself were regarded by Langulet as very delicate *morceaux.'*

The Parisian medical expert says that Langulet displayed something of the mannerism of a vampire in his desperate attempts to satisfy his appetite, which was clearly very much in excess of that which would be normal for a man of his size and weight. (He was about five feet ten inches tall and weighted a little under twelve stone.)

'He usually stayed indoors the whole of the day until sunset,' Dr Berthollet continues, 'when he would walk forth, and parade up and down the dirtiest lanes of Paris. And noting where a piece of stinking carrion lay floating in the kennel, he would return at midnight and, seizing it, convey it to his lodgings, and feast on it for the next day's meal.'

According to the Bicetre Archives, Langulet usually cooked this rotten meat over an open fire, which may well have gone some way to preventing him from contracting diseases. His constitution was also said to be incredibly strong; and he could apparently instantly tell the difference between the flesh of various animals. Later, however, his appetite began to demand new sensations, as Dr Berthollet reports.

'In this manner he kept up his wretched existence for years until, by a refinement in his appetite, he at length found his way to the burial grounds. He had determined to taste human flesh and with this in mind he had devised himself an ingenious instrument for the opening of graves. Although it required many attempts, he at length succeeded in pulling out of the graves several of the bodies recently interred. His appetite was so ravenous that he would feast upon the bodies on the spot, covering the remains with mould.'

Although it has proved impossible to establish exactly at which graveyard Langulet carried out his bizarre exhumations, it is believed to have been an old cemetery which once stood beside the rue de Clichy, a half hour walk from the tomb-robber's home. A Parisian tradition that a vampire once preyed upon unsuspecting victims at Trinité

Church on this same road may well have been inspired by Langulet's activities.

The urban cannibal apparently returned to the same tomb night after night, and would not dig up a fresh body until he had completely finished the current one. He would then meticulously bury the bones and leave no sign on the grave that it had been plundered. Langulet also took great care not to be seen entering or leaving the cemetery and only ever went there under cover of darkness.

'What is still more extraordinary,' say Dr Berthollet, 'is that he would feast himself upon the intestines in preference to any other part of the body. And when he had thus regaled himself, he would fill his pockets with as much as they would conveniently hold of this horrible material for a future meal.'

A Parisian tradition has it that Langulet was disturbed by a watchman one night while ransacking a grave and fled without having had a morsel to eat. In his desperation for food, he then attacked and murdered a prostitute and ate her flesh. However, the evidence of this crime is very circumstantial, and the girl may well have been dead before he found her and allegedly took several slices of flesh from her thighs. Certainly the body of a prostitute was found close to where Langulet lived shortly before he was apprehended in 1925 and there were signs that part of her body had been torn and eaten.

As Langulet's compulsion for flesh grew, says

Dr Berthollet, he decided to remove an entire body from one of the graves rather than eating it a bit at a time each night.

'He therefore determined on running the risk of discovery, and conveying his darling article of food to his lodging. This he attempted and actually conveyed at two such times, the whole of the body of a young female which had been entombed a week before. Here he was discovered regaling on this truly horrible repast; and the terrific appearance which the whole scene presented struck the beholders with unspeakable horror.'

The evidence suggests that although Langulet's neighbours knew of his bizarre appetite, they were so revolted at the idea of him eating putrefying flesh that no one wanted to go anywhere near him or his home. It was the discovery of a small item of female apparel outside his lodgings one morning in August 1825 that convinced a local resident the man's appetites had gone beyond animal flesh and he must now be eating the bodies of humans.

Langulet apparently allowed himself to be arrested without any kind of struggle, and he was taken to the Bicetre Prison. There he was seen by Dr Berthollet who continues his report:

'When interrogated on the subject of his dreadful depravity, Langulet said that from a child he had always been fond of what other people denominated loathsome food. He expressed his surprise and wonder that anyone could attach the least blame to him for a taste to him that was so natural. Nor did he appear to consider that he had committed any crime in endeavouring to satisfy that appetite in the way he had done.'

Dr Berthollet admitted in a preface to his report that he had expected to meet a raving lunatic and instead found himself confronted by a seemingly rational man driven by the most extraordinary compulsion for human flesh.

'His answers to whatever questions were put to him were precise and rational,' the doctor concluded his report, 'although there appeared at times a little incoherence in his manner. He acknowledges that he sometimes felt the greatest inclination to devour children of a tender age, but that he never could summon sufficient courage to kill them.'

Based on the doctor's report, the decision was taken that there was no point in putting Langulet on trial, but he should be kept in prison indefinitely, 'for fear of the consequences which might result from his horrible propensities'. Notwithstanding this, news of his nocturnal activities was soon common gossip all over Paris and became the subject of a number of sensational broadsheets and a song about 'The Man-Eater of Clichy'.

There was understandable scepticism about the grislier details of the story in some of the politer circles of Parisian society. But not long after it had begun publication in 1826, *Le Figaro* published a full account of the case of Antoine Langulet which it said 'had been the subject of much speculation'.

The paper's version, it said, had been 'communicated by Dr Berthollet and every reliance may be placed upon its authenticity.'

Despite his renown in his lifetime, today few people are familiar with the story of Langulet, the man who by a strange twist of fate shared the same locality as the Phantom of the Opera – but has shared none of his notoriety or fame.

The Gold-Rush Cannibals

Cannibalism was practised in America long before the coming of Christopher Columbus or, later, the white settlers from Europe. Quite a considerable number of the native Indian tribes included the eating of human flesh as part of their ceremonial and social customs, and many believed that the spirit of a brave fighter who had been killed in battle could be ingested through eating the man's heart.

There are, however, no hints of cannibalism to be found in those great classics about early American Indian history such as James Fenimore Cooper's *Last of the Mohicans* or Henry Wadsworth Longfellow's *Song of Hiawatha*. Yet the fact remains that certain tribes such as the Mohawks, the Hurons, the Dakota Indians and, most famously of all, the Kwakiutl Indians of the north-east Pacific coast, *did* practise cannibalism. The Kwakiutl are, indeed, famous for their fearsome spirit god with the mouthful of a name – Baxbakualanuxsiwae – which means literally 'He who is the First to eat Man at the Mouth of the River', and for the fact that under his patronage they become members of an élite group, the Hamatsas, who are free to eat the flesh of enemies and, should the necessity arise, even members of their own people.

The Kwakiutl are, in effect, licensed cannibals and despite many outside pressures have continued to maintain an affinity with their god by sharing his passion for human flesh. Although since the end of the nineteenth century the tribe has abandoned its annual ceremonial custom whereby each Hamatsas eats a mouthful of human flesh to acknowledge Baxbakualanuxsiwae, the act is still symbolised in a ritual dance in which the eating is done in mime.

Records indicate that it did not take the early settlers in the New World long to see the evidence of cannibalism among the Indians. In the seventeenth century, for instance, a Dutch clergyman reported that the Mohawks in the area now occupied by the city of Albany held religious cannibal feasts. 'The common people eat the arms, buttocks and trunk,' the man noted in his journal, 'but the chiefs eat the heads and the hearts.'

Another traveller from England at the same period of time saw flesh-eating among the Dakota Indians. 'When a warrior, after slaying a foe, eats, porcupine-like, the heart and liver, his purpose is to increase his own courage.' Similar accounts are also to be found in seventeenth- and eighteenth-century documents dealing with the customs of the Hurons and the Miamis.

One group which particularly inspired fear among the new emigrants was a tribe known as the Dueldeli-ottine (or 'Men of Blood') who lived in the Rocky Mountains near Fort Halkett. These people were said to be so used to experiencing famine that they routinely ate any parents, children and friends who died of hunger. They were quite prepared to eat any strangers who crossed their path, too, it was said.

But it would be wrong to imagine that it was only the Indians who resorted to cannibalism in America. Famine struck the new settlers, too, and there are a number of instances of travellers trapped in snowdrifts, lost in the mountains or in the vastness of the prairies who were forced to devour the flesh of companions who had died in order to save their own lives. A notable instance of this occurred in 1846 when a party of twenty-three vehicles carrying twenty-six men, fourteen women and forty-four children, lead by one George Donner, set out from Utah in August to battle their way through the Sierra Nevada Mountains to California. However, a terrible snowstorm enveloped the travellers as they neared the summit just before Christmas Day and, as they were unable to go on, their supplies soon ran out and there was no alternative but for the living to eat the flesh of the dead. Thirty-three days after the ordeal had begun, less than half the party were able to complete their harrowing trek to the Pacific coast.

Some of the newcomers even resorted to the practice under more normal circumstances, according to another of the early chroniclers, Captain John Smith. Writing in his book of *Travels*, he records the case of one early settler in Virginia who deliberately became a cannibal in 1610.

According to Captain Smith, one of the colonists in the newly-settled state had murdered his wife. He then salted her body – or 'powdered' it, to use the terminology of the time. Afterwards the man began to eat parts of his spouse before he was discovered by his horrified neighbours.

'Now whether she was better roasted, boiled or cabonado'd, I know not,' a Jamestown resident who had witnessed the events later told Captain Smith, 'but of such a dish as powdered wife, I never heard of!'

The legendary Mountain Men who first went into the unexplored western regions of the continent before the first settlers drove there in their wagon trains were also not above a little cannibalism to stay alive. Some, like the great Jeremiah Johnson, who lived in the early nineteenth century and has subsequently been celebrated in books and on film, lived off what they could catch on the land. But when this failed, they were forced to turn for their sustenance to the bodies of the Indians they had killed. According to legend, Jeremiah Johnson alone killed 247 Crow Indians and ate the livers of each and every one.

Probably the best documented evidence of cannibalism in the Old West comes from the era of the Gold Rush and occurred on the route to Pike's Peak, the mountain which overlooks Colorado Springs right in the heart of the United States. The details were first revealed by Henry Villard, a young newspaper correspondent, who joined the gold rush early in 1859 and sent back a number of dispatches to the *Cincinnati Daily Commercial*. Villard, who had been born in Germany and come to America as an eighteen-year-old in 1853, had worked on several newspapers, but it was his reports on the gold fever which gripped the Mid-West that brought him to national attention.

Interestingly, after leaving Pike's Peak and publishing the grisly details of what had occurred there, Villard experienced a spectacular rise to fame and fortune – becoming President of the Northern Pacific Railroad and a powerful figure in the financial world. However, he never forgot the story of what had happened in Colorado nor of meeting the gold-hunter who had survived extreme deprivation by resorting to cannibalism . . .

In the reports which he sent back to the *Cincinnati Daily Commercial*, Villard graphically described travelling across the vast plains of Kansas to Denver and then into the Rocky Mountains beyond. Here he found himself part of a large flow of humanity seeking what they hoped would be their Eldorado. One estimate put their numbers at their peak in excess of 10,000.

'They are of a most heterogeneous character,' he wrote. 'Indians of several tribes, Mexicans, mountaineers in buckskin, gold-hunters in flannel, blacklegs with stove-pipes, all can be seen about here. However, the loose state of society and the large influx of lawless individuals has already made resort to the lynch law necessary in this part of the country.'

But law-breaking – which the appropriately named Judge Lynch was doing his best to stem – was not the only cause of suffering in the district, as Villard wrote in one of his earliest reports in April 1859.

'Much misery has been, and is, experienced by many in crossing the plains and upon coming here,' he declared. 'The hand-cart and footing gentry had, and have, to pass through indescribable sufferings. Most of them started with an entirely insufficient stock of provisions, and if not starved before arriving, found themselves without the least particle of food upon coming in sight of the land of water and hope. As money is also a scarce article among most of them, starvation is their lot, from which to escape they resort to all possible means.'

Villard was able to see for himself some of the means used by these luckless gold-hunters to feed themselves, including selling off the very items of equipment they had brought to Pike's Peak in order to go prospecting.

'Every morning the rapidly articulating voice of

a backwoods auctioneer may be heard exerting his eloquence to the utmost in the attempt to find buyers for articles of outfit belonging to fundless gold-hunters,' Villard's report continued. 'Whole and tattered garments, picks, shovels, hand-carts, etc., can be bought in any quantities at mere nominal prices. Thus I was offered a good steel pick and shovel for twenty-five cents this morning. A hand-cart was sold in my presence for thirty-five cents. As a general rule everything, with the exception of provisions, can be bought at half the money it would cost in the rest of the States.

'A good many poor devils that landed here without anything either to eat or sell are at present hanging about the doors of those who are better provided with the necessaries of life, begging in the most pitiful terms for something to subsist on.'

A still more harrowing story awaited Henry Villard when his journey took him on to Pike's Peak. There he was shown a statement by Daniel Blue, a prospector who had been forced to eat the bodies of three fellow gold-hunters. Later, he came face to face with the man himself.

This man Blue, who had arrived full of hope from the town of Clyde in Whiteside County, Illinois in the spring of 1859, had apparently made the statement on 12 May at the office of the Leavenworth and Pike's Peak Express Company in Denver. In it, he described how he and his two brothers, Alexander and Charles Blue, along with two friends, John Campbell and Thomas Stevenson, had left the town of Clyde on 22 February intending to join the Pike's Peak gold rush. By 6 March, the five men has passed through Kansas City and were trekking along the Smoky Hill route. In the neighbourhood of Topeka, they were also joined by nine other prospectors all bound for western Kansas.

'The company had one horse.' Daniel Blue began his statement, 'which belonged to the original Blue party, and was to carry their provisions. The rest were footmen, carrying their provisions on their backs. We journeyed together for sixteen or seventeen days on the Smoky Hill route. Myself and eight others then continued our journey, while the rest remained behind for the purpose of hunting buffalo.'

After three or four days had elapsed the packhorse was lost, said Daniel Blue, and the group's stock of provisions was also very much reduced. The men decided to shoulder what was left and push onwards.

'After having travelled eight more days, two other members of the company left us,' his statement goes on. 'Upon their leaving our provisions became exhausted, and for ten days we laid still, endeavouring to kill a sufficient amount of game for our subsistence. A few hares, ravens and other small game was, however, all that came within our reach. Our only firearm was a shotgun, all the other arms having been thrown away in consequence of the weakness of their owners.

'At about the same time, three others parted from us with the intention of making for the nearest settlement for the purpose of securing relief to the remaining ones. This left but the three brothers Blue and one man by the name of Soleg from Cleveland, Ohio. All of the party were very weak and nearly exhausted.'

Things now began to go from bad to worse for the prospectors. Daniel Blue says that the men made another effort to continue their journey, but soon a combination of hunger and exhaustion compelled them to stop once again. The following day things looked really desperate. The party awoke the next morning to find the man Soleg on the point of dying from fatigue and inanition. At this point, Blue's statement takes on a 'blood-congealing tone', according to Henry Villard.

'Before he breathed his last, Soleg authorised and requested us to make use of his mortal remains in the way of nourishment,' the gold-hunter's document reads almost matter-of-factly. 'We, from necessity, did so, although it went very hard against our feelings. We lived on his body for about eight days.'

Daniel Blue goes into no more specifics about this first act of cannibalism, although it is believed that Soleg's flesh was roasted on a fire that the men made, while the offal and bones were used to make a soup when this was finished. It was not until some time later that the men would learn that they were then just about seventy-five miles east of Denver City at a place called Beaver Creek which empties into the Bijou, one of the tributaries of the South Platte River. Nor did their harrowing story end there.

'After the consumption of Soleg's body, Alexander, my eldest brother, died,' said Daniel Blue, 'and, at his own request, we used a portion of his body as food on the spot, and with the balance resumed our journey towards the gold regions.'

The two remaining men were now desperate-looking, their clothes hanging from their bodies and their eyes starting from their sockets. Together they covered another ten miles towards their destination before tragedy struck once more.

'This time it was my youngest brother Charles who gave out and we were obliged to stop,' Daniel Blue goes on. 'For ten days we subsided on what remained of our older brother's body, at which point Charles expired from the same causes as the others. I then consumed the greater portion of his remains. I had expected my fate to be the same as that of my brothers, but at the moment of despair I was unexpectedly found by an Arapahoe Indian and carried to his lodge where he treated me with the greatest kindness.'

Daniel Blue had escaped death by a hairbreadth, and after being fed and rested was taken by the Indian to the encampment of the Leavenworth and Pike's Peak Express Company. There he made his statement, 'freely, voluntarily and without compulsion, knowing that it will reach the eye of the public at large'.

Henry Villard pored over this statement, fascinated and revolted at one and the same time. He included the account verbatim in the next dispatch back to the newspaper in Cincinnati, but without embellishment or comment. There had been whispers before of cannibalism on the plains of Middle America, not to mention within sight of the gold fields, but this document amounted to the first voluntary confession by a man who had eaten the flesh of three other prospectors. Surprisingly, although the account was published in the *Daily Commercial* of 17 May this is the first retelling of the story in over a century and its first appearance in a book.

Henry Villard had one even more dramatic experience of the gold-hunting cannibal. While waiting to take a train on the next stage of his assignment, he unexpectedly came face to face with Daniel Blue himself. Once again he reported the event simply and objectively:

'Mr Blue came up to this place on the same coaches that I did,' he said afterwards. 'He looked like a skeleton, and could hardly use his limbs, and his sight was impaired.'

The journalist also had a salutary postscript to add to the Pike's Peak gold rush.

'I wish to remark,' he said, 'that in calling this the Pike's Peak gold region, a vast radical misnomer is made use of. From here to that much-mentioned glacier the distance comes not much short of seventy miles, and in but a single locality

143

between the two points gold-washing is carried on. And it does not pay. Any shovel full of sand will give the colour, but only the most diminutive substances of gold, and the idea of turning those all but invisible particles to account has been abandoned.'

In truth, the Eldorado that the Blue brothers had set out to find with such high hopes and which took two of their lives was just one more illusion in the gold fever that hit America in the middle of the nineteenth century . . .

Eliza Fraser and the Fatal Shore

As in America, cannibalism was already being practised in Australia long before Captain Cook made a landfall and began the opening up of that vast continent of three million square miles – huge tracts of which remain as mysterious and enigmatic today as they have done for countless centuries. The original inhabitants of the nation were the aborigines who had lived very much like Stone Age man until the arrival of the white men in the eighteenth century. Some, indeed, have steadfastly refused to change their ancient ways as a result of the influx of the newcomers, preferring their time-honoured customs and rituals.

Survival has always been a battle against the odds for the aborigines who lived for centuries without permanent dwellings and only a very basic knowledge of agriculture. Cannibalism had undoubtedly long been a part of their way of life, and may well have survived to this day among some of them in the very remote areas of the Northern Territory like Arnham Land, according to the anthropologist, Colin Simpson, who has written about them in his fascinating book, *Adam in Ochre* (1958).

Although Simpson is convinced that flesh-eating was not practised by the native Australians to the same extent as those natives in the South Sea Islands, he has discovered a number of specific examples which he cites:

'In hard summers, the new-born children were all eaten by the Kaura tribe in the neighbourhood of Adelaide,' he writes. 'In 1933 I was able to talk to old men who had eaten human flesh. The chief of Yam Island described to me how he had eaten finely-chopped man-meat mixed with crocodile-meat at his initiation. He added that it had made him sick. The purpose, as he put it, was "to make heart come strong inside".'

Simpson also learned that in the Wotjobaluk tribe a couple who already had a child might kill their new-born baby and feed its muscle-flesh to the other one in order to make it strong. The baby would be ritually killed by striking its head against the shoulder of its elder brother or sister, he was told.

'Human flesh-eating among many of the tribes was a sign of respect for the dead.' the anthropologist says. 'At a Dieri burial, for instance, relatives received, in strict order of precedence, small portions of the body-fat to eat. "We eat him," a tribesman said, "because we knew him and were fond of him." But sometimes the cannibalism was for revenge, and this is typified in the custom of the Ngarigo tribe who ate the flesh of the hands and feet of slain enemies, and accompanied the eating with loud expressions of contempt for the people killed.'

Blood rituals in which the blood of older men was anointed onto the bodies of young men or else given to them to drink in order to enhance their life, strength and courage have also been reported by other anthropologists from their study of the customs of the aborigines. One of them, A P Elkin of Sydney University, also discovered cannibalism occurring as part of their burial rites.

'Cannibalism forms part of the burial ceremony among many of the tribes of Queensland,' he wrote in 1961, 'and is considered a most honourable rite, to be used only for persons of worth, and proceeds the mummification of the body . . . The body would be dried over a fire or in the sun, after the internal organs had been removed through an incision, and then packed, bound up and, usually, painted. It is then made up into a bundle and carried around by the mourners until their grief has been assuaged. It is finally disposed of by interment, cremation or by being put inside a hollow tree. In some districts, the preparation is complicated by the cannibalism, so that the bundle consists only of the bones, or the bones and the dried skin.'

147

In another aboriginal tribe called the Wongkonguru, cannibalism was used as a means of detecting a suspected killer. If a member of the tribe had died suddenly, mysteriously or for no apparent reason, it was believed he had been 'boned' by an enemy. The way to discover the guilty party was to cook his body and then serve a piece of the flesh to anyone who might be a suspect. According to the tradition, the flesh would have no effect on the innocent but would poison the person who had 'boned' the dead man. It was a ritual that no aborigine would dare refuse, for as one tribe member put it, 'Spose me not eat 'em? Another fella say, Him kill 'em. Me eat 'em, then all right.'

But just as the Red Indians were not solely responsible for cannibalism in America, so the practice cannot be wholly ascribed to the Australian aborigines. Instances of flesh-eating are also to be found among the prisoners from England who were the continent's first reluctant residents and, after them, the emigrants who tried to make new lives for themselves in the daunting, hostile land 'down under'.

A typical story – though it is one that has curiously been little discussed – concerns an Irishman named Alexander Pierce who was transported to the country as a prisoner in 1820 and during two subsequent escapes was responsible for eating no fewer than four of his companions.

Pierce, who was born in County Fermanagh, was convicted of stealing six pairs of shoes and sentenced to be transported to Australia for seven years. There he was assigned to a succession of landowners from whom he stole or attempted to escape, and despite being repeatedly captured and lashed as many as fifty times, he continued to commit crimes until he was finally sent to the Penal settlement of Macquarie Harbour. Even this fearsome and reputedly escape-proof prison proved unable to hold the Irishman, however, as a statement he later gave to the magistrates at Hobart reveals.

'I was not there more than a month before I made my escape with seven others,' Pierce said, 'namely Dalton, Traverse, Badman, Mathews, Greenhill, Brown and Cornelius. We kept together for ten days, during which time we had no food but our kangaroo-skin jackets which we ate, being nearly exhausted, with hunger and fatigue. On the eleventh night we began to consult what was best to be done for our preservation, and made up our minds to a dreadful result.'

Pierce and his companions had decided to eat one of their number, he explains, though not every one of the group was prepared to be a party to the plan.

'In the morning we missed three of our companions, Dalton, Cornelius and Brown, who we concluded had left us with the intention of going back if possible. We then drew cuts which of us five should die and it fell to Badman's lot. I went with one of the others to collect dry wood and make a fire during which time Traverse had succeeded in killing Badman and had begun to cut him up. We dressed part of the flesh immediately, and continued to use it as long as it lasted.

'We then drew cuts again, and it fell to the fate of Mathews. Traverse and Greenhill killed him with an axe, cut the flesh from his bones, carried it on, and lived upon it as long as it lasted. By the time it was all eaten, Traverse through fatigue fell lame in his knee, so much so that he could not proceed. Greenhill proposed that I should kill him, which I agreed to do. We then made the best of our way, carrying the flesh of Traverse between us, in the hope of reaching the Eastern settlements while it lasted.'

But despite setting themselves a punishing pace, the two men seemed forever lost in the wilderness and getting no closer to their destination. Pierce was also becoming very uneasy about his companion.

'I perceived the Greenhill always carried the axe,' he stated later, 'and thought he was waiting an opportunity to kill me. I was always on my guard, though, and finally succeeded when he fell asleep to get hold of the axe with which I immediately despatched him and made a meal. I then carried the remaining flesh with me to feed upon.'

Finally, when even this human flesh ran out, Pierce was forced to keep himself alive on grass and nettle-tops. He was just on the point of collapse when he luckily stumbled upon what had evidently been an aboriginal resting place and there found some entrails and bits of kangaroo which he gratefully gobbled up. He had now, he said, had enough of his nomadic life and decided to give himself up. Within a week he was back in the penal settlement at Macquarie Harbour, having lied successfully about the real fate of the other escapers.

But Pierce had obviously still not learned his lesson, and once more he escaped from the colony with another man named Thomas Cox. The breakout was made despite the fact that Pierce was in leg-irons, and he was not able to remove these until the pair had travelled several excruciatingly painful miles and Cox had the time to use an axe which he had stolen from the camp. This, though, was not the end of their suffering.

'We travelled on several miles without food, except the tops of trees and shrubs, until we came to King's River,' said Pierce. 'I asked Cox if he could swim and he replied that he could not. I remarked that had I been aware of this he should not have been my companion. We made a fire and while arranging how we should cross the river we had words. I then killed Cox with the axe and ate part of him that night. The greater part of the flesh I cut up in order to take with me.

'The next morning I swam the river with the intention of keeping to the coast round to Port Dalrymple. But my heart failed me and I resolved to return and give myself up to the Commandant. I

151

threw most of the flesh away, but one piece, which I carried in my pocket to show the Commandant that Cox was dead. I confessed that I had killed him and accompanied a party in a boat to bring up his remains, which was done.'

Even in the harsh and brutal world of the new colony, Alexander Pierce's confession which he made when brought before the magistrates in the Court House in Hobart on 6 July 1824 caused widespread revulsion and horror. The Irishman was quite unashamed about his cannibalism, claiming it was the only way he could have survived. He received the death penalty with an equal lack of emotion.

Gruesome as Pierce's story is, it earned none of the notoriety or fame that surrounded Eliza Fraser's escape from cannibals in 1836 on the 'Fatal Shore' – as Australia was popularly known at the time.

Eliza, born in Orkney, Scotland, was the attractive, thirty-seven-year-old wife of a Captain Fraser who set sail with her and a crew of twenty aboard the *Stirling Castle* from Sydney bound for New Guinea around Australia's Pacific coast. That Eliza was making the trip at all was remarkable, for she was heavily pregnant and expected the baby to be born only hours after the ship was due to reach its destination.

However, the vessel had hardly left harbour when a terrible storm blew up and Captain Fraser was forced to order his wife and crew to abandon ship in the *Stirling Castle's* two lifeboats. The first was lost almost immediately, but the Captain and his wife fared rather better and managed to keep afloat as they struggled towards the shore. Amidst this deluge of foam and wind, Eliza unexpectedly gave birth to her child, which did not survive long.

Several terrifying hours later the exhausted survivors of the *Stirling Castle* were cast up on to dry land at Botany Bay. But they had only escaped one appalling situation to fall into another, for as the later report states, they were immediately seized by a tribe of aborigines known as the Kabi and dragged off to their settlement.

The previous day's storm had not only all but drowned the seamen, but stripped off most of their clothes. Eliza apparently had only a 'sou'w-ester and figleaf of flowering sea-grapes to conceal her modesty', but still did her best to maintain her dignity. She even kept up her resolution when being beaten and burned by the natives as well as used as target practice by their children learning to throw boomerangs. Captain Fraser, incensed at what was being done to his wife, tried to intervene but was savagely hacked down and killed by a spear.

For several weeks Eliza Fraser battled to survive the cruelties of the natives and the hostility of her environment. She was forced in her almost naked state to raid wild bees' nests for honey, dive for lily bulbs and grub for roots while being bitten by hordes of the vicious Pacific coast insects. As if this was not horrifying enough, she even had to sit by and watch several members of the crew being killed and eaten by the Kabi. After each killing, she was also forced to taste the heart and liver of the dead man.

Pure chance lead to Eliza Fraser's rescue. A ship manned by a convict crew happened to stop in Botany Bay and, while taking on water, an army lieutenant in charge of the prisoners noticed a pale skin amongst the black figures squatting at one end of the beach. Intrigued, he approached the group and, seeing the semi-naked woman among the aborigines, 'literally talked Mrs Fraser out of the encampment and into the rescue boat,' to quote a contemporary account.

Eliza Fraser's great resilience had obviously enabled her to survive her ordeal – and the enforced cannibalism – and as soon as she was back in Sydney she quickly became a celebrity. She became the subject of stories in the newspapers; a guest at every fashionable gathering; and was enriched by a collection made to help her overcome her ordeal in excess of $1,000.

Realising she might profit further from her adventure, Eliza set sail for her native country in February 1837. And on the way home, she so charmed the captain of the *Mediterranean Packet*, Alexander John Greene, that they were man and wife before the ship docked in London. Once again she became the toast of the town – celebrated in newspaper articles, penny broadsheets and popular songs – and was also the recipient of another £553 from a public subscription launched by the admiring Lord Mayor of London.

For a time it was said Eliza even exhibited herself in Hyde Park in a booth which was decorated with a large picture of some savages busy cutting up and eating the corpses of a number of white men and women roasting over a huge fire. Underneath was the sign: 'The *Stirling Castle* wrecked off the coast of Botany Bay all killed and eaten by savages. Only survivor a woman – to be seen for 6d admission.'

Some mystery surrounds this sideshow, however, for one persistent rumour said that Eliza had already returned to Australia with her husband to enjoy the wealth her experience had earned her, and the booth contained an impostor put there by an unscupulous showman – of which London boasted not a few at the time.

In any event, Eliza Fraser never made the headlines again in either Britain or Australia, living out the remaining years of her life quietly and uneventfully in Melbourne as a good wife and mother. At the end, the woman who had survived a shipwreck, the birth of a child in the midst of a storm, and living with a tribe of cannibals, died prosaically as a result of a carriage accident while crossing the street.

'The Custom of the Sea'

In the eighteenth century, cannibalism at sea was almost routine amongst sailors who were shipwrecked and ran out of provisions. Indeed, the practice became euphemistically known as 'the Custom of the Sea', and in a number of countries was virtually regarded as legitimate as long as some means of chance – such as drawing straws or throwing dice – had been used beforehand to decide who was to be eaten.

However, this curious example of maritime democracy as a prerequisite to eating flesh was not *quite* as fair as it might seem. For records indicate that in the majority of instances it was the smallest member of the shipwrecked crew, usually the cabin boy, who ended up being eaten. And there are few more graphic examples of this than the story of Richard Park, the seventeen-year-old English cabin boy of a thirty-one-ton yacht, the *Mignonette*, who was killed and eaten by the Captain and surviving crew members after their vessel sank and they had all taken to an open lifeboat in the summer of 1884.

Though the horror of the *Mignonette* is far from an isolated case in maritime history, it is particularly notable in that when two of the men who survived the ordeal were brought to trial, they became the first British subjects in legal history to stand charged with murder for this offence in open court.

The events of the case, which unfolded when the men appeared at the Cornwall Winter Assizes at Exeter in November 1884, provide one of the most detailed and authentic accounts of cannibalism at sea. They were charged with having 'killed and eaten the cabin boy in order to save their own lives when they were in dire distress from starvation'. It was a case that caused a sensation in Victorian Britain.

As far as the public were concerned, the story began on 6 September 1884 when a German merchantman, the *Montezuma*, docked at Falmouth at the end of a trans-atlantic voyage from Punta Arenas in Chile. On board as unexpected passengers were three haggard, wild-eyed seamen, Captain Thomas Dudley, aged thirty-one, and two members of his crew, the first mate, Edwin Stephens (thirty-six), and seaman Edmund Brooks (thirty-nine). All had apparently been rescued from the sea during the voyage and had a very sorry tale to tell.

Captain Dudley, it transpired, had been commissioned to sail the *Mignonette*, a cutter-rigged vessel of thirty-three tons built originally in 1867 at Brightlingsea in Essex, from Southampton to Sydney, New South Wales, where she was to be handed over to her new owner, a Mr Henry J Want. For the voyage he had hired a crew of three – Stephens, Brooks and the teenager, Richard Parker. The craft left Southampton on the morning tide of 19 May and the journey south had initially proceeded uneventfully, with the *Mignonette* crossing the equator on 17 June.

However, as July arrived the weather worsened dramatically. Storms lashed the boat for three days and Captain Dudley and the crew had to struggle to keep her afloat. Then on 5 July, about 1,600 miles from the Cape of Good Hope – the actual position was 27S 10W – the vessel had finally taken on so much water that the pump could no longer cope. Captain Dudley ordered the men to abandon ship.

The tiny open boat into which the four men climbed was ill-equipped to support a shipwreck party. There was no ready supply of water and no food other than two 1lb tins of vegetables. There was also very little in the way of cover to protect the men from the elements.

The awful events which occurred in the following days until the survivors were rescued on 29 July, having drifted for almost a 1,000 miles to 24S, 27W, were related first to their rescuers on the *Montezuma* and then to the custom-house authorities at Falmouth. None of the men had made any attempt to deny what had occurred in the lonely reaches of the Atlantic Ocean.

There was some sympathy for the crew of the *Mignonette* from the men on the German ship who knew about hunger at sea and what it could make a man do. But after they had repeated their story of killing and eating the young cabin boy for a third time to the police authorities in Falmouth, a decision was made to press charges. Only Edmund Brooks, it was decided, was exempted from the court appearance on 6 November, having satisfied the law that he had made several attempts to resist the proposed cannibalism. The case itself caused as much perplexity in legal circles as it did curiosity amongst members of the public, who crowded into the courtroom to hear the proceedings held before Mr Baron Huddlestone.

The greatest interest, of course, focused on the events which had occurred after the shipwreck. According to the evidence presented in court, the captain had failed to appreciate the gravity of the situation in which the men found themselves and did nothing to eke out the meagre resources, and the two tins of vegetables quickly ran out. Although a small turtle was caught on the fourth day, which provided subsistence for a little longer, by the twelfth day there was nothing to eat whatsoever. The only fresh water the men were able to obtain came from catching a few drops of rain in their oilskin capes.

For eight days the little boat drifted helplessly on

the tides. By now all four had the shrunken look of desperate men as they battled against hunger and thirst. It was Captain Dudley who first voiced what the others had not dared to say – for all three knew about 'The Custom of the Sea'. Staring at the figure of the cabin boy who for some time had been lying prostrate and semi-conscious in the bottom of the boat, he finally spoke.

'It would be better that one should die than all should perish,' he said hoarsely between lips that were cracked and split.

At this Edmund Brooks looked up with agonised eyes. 'No, no,' he was reported to have said. 'I cannot consent to such a proposal. If God wills that we should die by starvation, let us submit to His decree. I shall be no party to the shedding of blood.'

The outburst seemed to calm the fevered minds of the other two, but the following day Captain Dudley spoke again – now suggesting that lots should be drawn for the one who was to be sacrificed. Again Brooks refused to be any part of such a plan. He was to state later that at no time was the increasingly delirious cabin boy consulted about the idea.

At nightfall, the captain returned to the subject a third time. Though his voice was little more than a croak, there was a deeper note of conviction in it. This time he only spoke directly to the first mate, Edwin Stephens.

'Ned, you and I are married men,' he said, 'with

families of our own. It is not right that we should die while there is a possibility of life and thus leave our dear ones to the mercy of a pitiless world.'

The other man narrowed his salt-encrusted eyes. 'You are right, Captain,' he replied. 'My children are unprovided for. It is our duty to look after our own, no matter at what sacrifice.'

Brooks, who it was later learned in court was unmarried, was apparently asleep during this exchange, and heard nothing of the agreement the two men made.

'It is no use mentioning the matter to Brooks,' Captain Dudley was alleged to have said, 'he will never give in. We must take the whole burden upon ourselves. Poor Parker can scarcely hold out for another day, and it would be a blessing to put him out of his misery.'

Stephens nodded his head and asked if the boy should be told of his fate.

'No, I think not,' the captain went on. 'It would only disturb his mind. Tonight we shall give him respite, but if no sail should heave into sight before tomorrow morning, the poor fellow must die to save us. It will only be anticipating his certain fate by a few hours, and neither God nor man can blame us for an act to which we are driven in our direst extremity.'

Neither man apparently spoke again during the night as they looked in vain for help. Then as dawn crept over the horizon, the cabin boy suddenly rolled over on to his side and in a frenzy

161

began drinking some of the sea water that had been shipped during the night. The captain and first mate looked at each other – they sensed, they said later, that madness and death was very close to the cabin boy.

Dudley took a small penknife from his waterproof jacket pocket and felt the blade. He turned to his companion.

'Ned,' he whispered, 'if he should struggle, will you hold his legs?'

And without waiting for an answer, he turned to the third man, who was just stirring.

'Brooks, you had better go back to sleep.'

This time the older man knew from the look in the captain's eyes that any protest would be in vain.

Dudley now moved to the side of the prostate cabin boy. 'Dick, my boy,' he said quietly, 'your end has come.'

Richard Parker's eyes suddenly opened wide with fear and his voice struggled to escape from his parched and distended throat. 'Not me, sir!' he croaked, 'Not me, sir! Oh, don't!'

But before the lad could finish the sentence, Dudley had struck. His penknife penetrated Parker's throat and the jugular vein was severed. The boy died without another sound.

What followed has been graphically recorded by an observer who attended the trial in Falmouth and noted down the evidence.

'Then, we were told, was enacted a most horrible performance,' the account states, 'Stephens, the mate, dragged himself forward with the two empty vegetable tins, and the life-blood of Parker was caught as it ran, the men drinking in turns as each vessel filled. Even Brooks could not resist the temptation of the dreadful draught, hot and red from the flowing veins, but drank with the rest till their faces were all bedabbled and smeared, and they looked like vampires at their unholy orgy.

'When their thirst was quenched, they stripped the body of the boy of all its clothing, and from the fleshy part of the thighs – now lean enough after twenty days' starvation – they cut off sufficient to appease their hunger. Brooks also made no demur now that the deed was done. He had served his conscience by protesting against the act, so he feasted with his comrades at the human banquet until satisfied. For four long days Parker's flesh kept them alive. They ate but sparingly, not knowing how long they might have to exist upon the awful fare, which they were compelled to devour raw, not having any means by which they might cook the flesh.'

Finally, on the fourth day, the *Montezuma* hove into sight. Only Brooks apparently had the strength to stand upright in the little boat and hail the German merchantman. The captain and mate appeared slumped in a kind of stupor, unable to rise, and had to be slung in ropes to be hauled on board by their rescuers.

It was to be some time before any of the three could speak about what had happened. And if their confession startled the men of the *Monte-zuma*, it was nothing to the effect it had upon the judge and jury listening at the Assizes. Seamen might have heard of such things before, but to those who lived on land cannibalism at sea was only the darkest rumour.

Baron Huddlestone, who had tried to sit impassively during this catalogue of horrors, felt that only one course of action was open to him and the jury. He directed the twelve good men and true that they should find 'a special verdict', leaving it to a higher court to decide what crime – if any – had been committed. The jury accepted this direction, declaring their ignorance as to whether 'murder had been done' and referred the matter to the Royal Courts of Justice. The accused were granted bail in their own surety of £100 plus another in the same amount.

Interest in the case was at a fever pitch when the proceedings opened again in London at the Court of the Queen's Bench. The case was then reheard by five judges, Lord Chief Justice Coleridge, Mr Justice Grove, Mr Justice Denman, Mr Baron Pollock and, for a second time, by Mr Baron Huddlestone. The Crown was represented by Sir Henry James and the defence by Mr Collins QC.

Another account of these proceedings reveals the dilemma in which the judges found themselves as the horror of the *Mignonette* was repeated.

'The judges listened to the whole terrible story

with knitted brows, and then fell to arguing,' the report states. 'They argued with counsel and argued amongst themselves for the whole of that day. At length, the Lord Chief Justice announced that they would give judgement later in the week. Mr Collins, who defended the prisoners, applied for bail as before, but this was not agreed to, and the two men were conducted to Holloway to await their Lordships' decision.

'It was not, in fact, until Tuesday, 9 December that final judgement was given. For the first time for more than a hundred years, the death sentence was that day heard in the Court of the Queen's Bench. The judgement read by Lord Coleridge was of exceeding length, but suffice it to say the two prisoners were found guilty of murder and sentenced to death. There was, however, a strong recommendation for mercy, in which the judges concurred.'

The division of the public's view about this act of cannibalism was to be heard on every street corner, in every public house and restaurant, and in column after column in the daily newspapers. To some it had been a brutal act of savagery on a defenceless boy, to others the act of dying men with no other course of action.

On 13 December, it was announced that Captain Dudley and first mate Edwin Stephens were to be reprieved. The Home Secretary, Sir William Harcourt, had studied the trial proceedings and decided to act upon the judges' recommendation.

He commuted the sentences to one of six months' imprisonment without hard labour.

In the summer of 1885, Thomas Dudley and Edwin Stephens quietly left Holloway Prison and were never heard of again. Neither ever returned to the sea, and both were said to have never touched meat again. Only Edmund Brooks returned to his former profession, though he refused to sign for any cruise that went beyond British waters.

The story of the killing of the *Mignonette*'s cabin boy was far from the last instance of cannibalism at sea, however. Even as recently as 1988, a boat-load of South Vietnamese refugees adrift in a leaking vessel began to kill and eat each other when starvation set in. According to the evidence, four people – including two children aged eleven and fourteen – were beheaded, dismembered and their flesh cooked and eaten by the others in the boat.

It would appear that 'The Custom on the Sea' is far from over . . .

The Bread and Butter Brides

Georg Karl Grossmann was a familiar figure at the Silesian railway terminus in Berlin during the years immediately after the First World War. From dawn in the morning until often quite late at night, he ran a little stall selling hot sausages and cold meats to the thousands of hungry travellers who poured through the noisy, smoke-filled station.

Few of those who stopped to buy a snack at Grossmann's stall gave him more than a passing glance, however. Most just selected a snack, paid for it, and then hurried on to catch a train or make their way home. The customer with the time – or inclination – to stop and eat their purchase in front of the stall was a rarity. In truth, Grossmann was, like his name, a big, surly fellow who liked to keep himself to himself. He usually stood impassively behind the trays of meat and hot-dogs, replenishing them almost as quickly as they were emptied.

Although Grossmann was only in his early

167

fifties he had the haunted look of a man who was much older. He had a round, pale face with dark, listless eyes which were made to appear even more gloomy by a ragged, droopy moustache. He rarely smiled and even more rarely exchanged anything other than the most perfunctory remark with his customers. If the hot-dog seller enjoyed his job – or got any satisfaction from it – he made a pretty good job of concealing the fact, some of his customers were to recall later when the gruesome truth about his other, secret life, and what he put into his wares, finally came to light.

German criminal records indicate that Georg Karl Grossmann was born in the town of Neuruppin, about thirty miles to the north of Berlin, in 1863. His father was a butcher and he, too, trained in the same profession. He was apparently an overweight, rather disagreeable child with a persistent eye-twitch which made looking into his face for any length of time a rather disconcerting experience. Indeed, his appearance probably explains why he preferred working in the back room of the family shop, cutting the joints and making the sausages, while his parents served the customers at the front.

By the time he was in his twenties, Georg Karl Grossmann was displaying some unpleasant tendencies. He was undoubtedly a sadist and began to prey on young children. He also tried to lure young girls with the offer of free meat from the family shop, and also occasionally indulged in bestiality. By the time the First World War broke out, he had served three terms of imprisonment and moved from Neuruppin to Berlin.

Because of his police record, Grossmann was not called up into the services. Instead, he continued to work as a butcher and during the hard times of the war used his access to meat to serve his perverted needs. Older women were his primary interest now and he also began to regularly use prostitutes.

By the end of the war, Grossmann was a thorough-going degenerate, and had also established a new business that would enable him to combine his eye for commerce with satisfying his unnatural lusts. He had realised that whatever else happened, there would always be a ready flow of people wanting feeding at the Berlin stations. So he negotiated for a good situation at the busy Silesian terminus, set up a stall and tapped his old contacts in the meat trade for his supplies.

For a time it seems that Georg Karl Grossmann ran his business with a degree of honesty. In order to make his sausages go further he added bread and minced vegetables to the mixture; and whenever meat was in short supply he would butcher small animals such as stray dogs and cats to augment his wares. Always, though, the food was invitingly presented, and in the hustle and bustle of the station few people probably had the time – or the inclination – to return and make a complaint about a sausage that seemed to have a flavour of turnip about it or a piece of meat that didn't quite taste like beef. And in those hard days, of course, there was very little flavour in a great deal of German food . . .

Within a couple of years, however, Georg Grossmann's sausages had earned quite a reputation. Now always plump and juicy, they were richly-flavoured and many a customer found an unmistakable trace of blood when they were bitten into or sliced. That Grossmann obviously had a good supplier of fresh meat was the opinion of those who used the stall regularly.

It was at this time, too, that the bulky stall-holder was first observed deviating from his normal habits. Instead of appearing behind the stall every day, he took to closing up for the odd day once every fortnight or so. As he was making a good living it was assumed that Grossmann could afford the time off, his customers decided slightly enviously when they called at the stall only to find it closed and shuttered.

But actually, instead of taking a day off to rest in his flat near the railway terminus, Grossmann was returning stealthily to the station. And it was to be some time before anyone noticed him – *or* what he was doing.

In fact, Grossmann was circling the platforms where the long-distance trains from the furthest corners of Germany ended their journeys. From out of these trains – in particular the cheap fourth-class carriages – poured a stream of desperate men and women from the provinces, all hoping that

Berlin might provide their crock of gold. Quite a few of the passengers were pretty girls dreaming that the big city might offer romance as well as a job.

The casual observer could have been excused for thinking that the bulky figure hunched in a coat sitting on a bench watching the stream of humanity was a harmless voyeur. Certainly he looked at the women with a great deal of interest, his twitching eye becoming more agitated whenever a pretty face caught his interest. His purpose, though, was anything but innocent.

Grossmann was especially interested in girls who were buxom and plump, it transpired later when he was arrested. His interest was particularly keen for those who alighted from the fourth-class carriages clutching belongings under their arms and with the lost look in their eyes of someone seeking a new life. He would then approach these girls deferentially and, with a polite doff of his hat, enquire if he could be of any assistance.

Even someone as unattractive as Georg Karl Grossmann must have seemed like a godsend to a bewildered girl from rural Germany who had most likely never seen a big city before. And if his appearance was a bit off-putting, it certainly did nothing to suggest the kind of dangers represented by the smartly-dressed, smooth-tongued city men about whom these girls had probably been warned.

Courteously enquiring about the girl's plans in

Berlin, Grossmann would listen with interest and if, as he had correctly surmised, the girl was looking for work, he would express the greatest surprise. What a coincidence, he had actually been on his way across the station to an agency in the hope of securing the services of a housekeeper! Fate must have thrown them together!

Then as he carefully tried to master his twitch, Grossmann would politely tell the girl that he had a bachelor apartment nearby and needed someone to keep it clean and tidy and do a little cooking now and then. It would not be a very arduous job, he insisted, and he paid well. No doubt smiling appreciatively at his victim's ample proportions, he would add that she seemed ideal for his purposes and that the job was hers for the asking.

There is evidence that not every lonely young girl who arrived at the Silesian terminus fell for this line. But during the years he had the stall at the station – from 1915 to 1921 – there were certainly plenty who did: and none was ever seen again after Grossmann had escorted them back to his flat. For there they were kept for probably no more than a couple of days, during which time they were sexually abused and then brutally murdered.

Grossmann's skill as a butcher made it a simple task for him to dismember the corpses in his kitchen. He would pare off the flesh and put it in bags and then methodically dispose of the bones in the nearby sewers or the river. Later he would pickle the flesh, grind it up, and mix it in the normal mincemeat as the filling for his sausages.

These delicacies he sold by the hundred, even the thousands, to the unsuspecting travellers of Berlin.

Quite how many girls Grossmann lured to their deaths in his flat has proved impossible to determine. Because he never used the same platform twice in succession and avoided luring females from similar destinations, the police were unable to decide from amongst all the young girls who had arrived by train in Berlin and then disappeared, just which ones might have been his victims. Some had undoubtedly wanted to disappear after running away from home and subsequently had become involved in prostitution and drugs; while others were just as likely to have fallen victim to the violence which was everywhere in the underworld of the city at that time.

Nor did the hot-dog killer only prey on girls from out of town. His appetite for prostitutes was undiminished and these he also took to his flat where they suffered a similar fate. The killing of the prostitutes was later to give the case its popular description, *Die Bräute auf der Stulle* – The Bread and Butter Brides – since any girl who slept with a client overnight was known in Germany at that time as a 'bride'.

There seems little doubt that Grossmann was also able to conceal his grisly activities because of the conditions in Berlin at the time. The fact that food was still scarce made hungry people less inclined to question the ingredients of the snacks they bought from stalls like his. And his ground-floor flat was also ideal for someone who did not want to be seen coming and going: it had a separate entrance and Grossmann always paid the landlord at the front door, never allowing him in.

But although Grossmann was careful in all his sorties after girls, he could not hope to escape entirely the curious eyes of his neighbours. Because he was a bachelor and had what was seen as a good business, it was not surprising that he should be seen taking girls regularly into his flat. Whores, all of them, the neighbours would whisper, because what decent girl would fancy a surly old man like that with his dreadful twitch? The fact that the girls were only ever seen once seemed to add weight to this theory. And even the odd cry in the night from the darkened flat was just put down to Grossmann's sexual proclivities.

It was not until the spring of 1921 that the first signs were noticed that Georg Karl Grossmann might be up to something a little more sinister than just entertaining prostitutes in his flat. A girl, naked and clearly terrified, was seen briefly at a window looking as if she was trying to attract attention. Then one of the drains from Grossmann's flat was observed to be overflowing with a red substance which looked remarkably like blood. A couple of his neighbours decided to have a quiet word with the police.

Then after another report that the bulky hot-dog vendor had brought home a girl carrying a large suitcase whom no one had seen leaving the flat, the authorities decided that the time had come to investigate. A search warrant was obtained and as Grossmann returned home from work the following evening he was unceremoniously grabbed and bundled into the flat.

Inside, the policemen found a scene of horror. Lying on a camp bed was the body of a girl, quite clearly dead. She showed every sign of having been brutally raped and then stabbed. The corpse had also been trussed up in the manner of a carcass in a slaughter house. It was as if she had been made ready for butchering, the officers thought.

In the kitchen, the policemen also found several trays of what at first looked like sausage meat. And in a cupboard another searcher came across a bundle of female clothing. The labels on several of these garments subsequently proved that they had belonged to girls reported missing after arriving at the Silesian station. In all, the horrified officers found enough remains to indicate that at least three women had been killed and dismembered in the flat during the past month.

Taken to police headquarters, the surly Grossmann was interrogated for several hours before finally beginning to admit to his terrible trade in human flesh. His confession about how he had stripped the skin and fat from the bodies of his victims and cooked it for his meat products made two officers physically sick.

As soon as these grisly details emerged, a group

of policemen with rather stronger stomachs were hastily dispatched to the Silesian station to remove Grossmann's stall and everything on it before the public got to hear about what precisely had been in the hot-dogs and cold meats which they had so enjoyed.

Grossmann's subsequent trial appalled even the war-hardened citizens of Berlin. It lasted for just three days and the defendant was found guilty of the murder of two of the girls whose remains had been identified in his flat. When the death sentence was pronounced on him he merely burst into laughter, according to a contemporary newspaper report.

During Grossmann's confinement in gaol awaiting execution he had several fits of mania. Not once, though, did he express any remorse for the girls he had murdered, whose number may have totalled as many as fifty. In the end he even cheated the gallows, for when the guards entered his cell just twenty-four hours before he was due to die they found him hanging from the ceiling.

No further remains of any of Georg Karl Grossmann's other victims were ever found – and it was said that for a year after his trial not a single slice of cold meat or a hot-dog was sold in the Silesian terminus . . .

The White Cannibal of New York

In all the annals of cannibalism, the most curious tale of a self-confessed flesh-eater is probably that of William Seabrook, an American-born former journalist and explorer, who actually wrote a report of his grisly feast. It remains to this day probably the most authentic account of eating human flesh by a man innocent of shedding blood or committing murder in order to experience the sensation.

Seabrook, a tall, dark and handsome man who bore a striking resemblance to the young Clark Gable, lived a wildly adventurous life which eventually burned him out physically and mentally before he was sixty. He sought excitement and sensation in many corners of the world. Several times he only just escaped with his life from the hands of murderous African natives and, later, experimented dangerously with huge amounts of drugs in India and the Far East which very nearly killed him. For years his most famous exploit was taking part in some secret voodoo rites. The most famous, that is, until he became a twentieth-century cannibal in South America just over sixty years ago.

Seabrook was born to comfortably-off parents in the year 1886 in the Maryland city of Westminster, not far from Baltimore. His early career as a journalist was apparently fairly unremarkable, until the late twenties when he was dispatched abroad by his editor to be a foreign correspondent. By 1934, his taste for adventure and exploration had grown to such an extent that he threw up this regular job and set out to find the exotic peoples and places he would subsequently write about in such graphic detail in books with titles like *Voodoo Island* (1936), *Jungle Ways* (1938) and *Magic and Witchcraft* (1940). Even a bout of alcoholism which confined him to hospital for seven months and which he subsequently described in *Asylum* (1935) did nothing to dampen his craving for excitement.

Seabrook's explorations took him to Arabia, Kurdistan, Africa and Haiti – among many other places – all of these trips into hostile environments funded by the sales of his books. He was never afraid of a challenge and on at least three occasions went alone with only a native guide into parts of the world where white men had never been seen before. It was on one of these trips to the interior of South America in 1938 that he first had the opportunity to discuss cannibalism with a native warrior and, later, to actually taste the flesh of a recently-killed man.

Seabrook had been living with a tribe known as the Guere for several weeks before he found a suitable opportunity to ask the chief if he had ever 'eaten white meat'.

'He looked at me quizzically and laughed, as if it were as good a joke as any,' the explorer wrote later. 'He said he had eaten it rarely in his youth, and hadn't tasted it for nearly twenty years; that it tasted exactly like the meat of the black men and was no better. Anyway, he added with another grin, the whites had always been too difficult to catch, and they made too many bothersome histories about it afterwards. So it really wasn't worth the bother. White man's meat tasted in no way different, he repeated, from the meat of the black man.'

But what, Seabrook persisted, did it really *taste* like? He told the old chief that he had heard and read many stories – always second-hand, of course – in which human flesh was said to 'look and smell and taste like pork'. But though he felt there was probably an element of truth in this, he was not convinced.

'The chief's replies, alas, were not very illuminating,' Seabrook continued. 'They were frank, but not instructive. He said with conviction that it was "very good meat", and, seeing that I was still not satisfied, insisted with even stronger conviction that "it is as good meat as any, and is considered by some people to be the best meat of all."

Decidedly that didn't help any. It was even less instructive than the books and tales which I had scorned. And since I didn't entirely scorn them, but had in mind their theoretical probability, I said, to help him toward some possible comparison, "Have you ever eaten pork?" I continued, "Does it taste anything like pork?" To which he replied, "But it tastes nothing like pork. It isn't like pork at all. It isn't the same thing at all. We have pigs here in the village. I have often eaten pork. It is not anything like that."'

Still Seabrook would not give up. What flesh did it most resemble, then? Goat, or sheep, or beef or even dog?

'He puzzled over it, shaking his head. He had no answer and got perhaps a little bored by my interminable questions. Obviously there was only one thing to do, if I ever could, and I didn't yet know him well enough or trust my guide's discretion sufficiently to broach my wish directly. But I just *had* to find out for myself.'

William Seabrook had set himself seemingly impossible tasks before. But nothing, he would recall later, represented such a challenge as eating human flesh, especially as he had no wish for anyone to be killed to satisfy his morbid curiosity. Yet the fact that there was one of those rare mysteries that deserved solving drove him on.

It was to be some little time, in fact, before a suitable opportunity arose – and under circumstances which he has understandably not described in too much detail. His account is unique as far as I know and has not been in print for over half a century. It is not recommended to those of a queasy nature:

'The occasion was one which would probably never be repeated, so that I felt in duty bound to make the most of it. In addition, therefore, a portion of stew with rice – sure to be highly seasoned with red pepper that fine shades of flavour might be lost to an unaccustomed palate – I had requested and been given a sizeable rump steak, also a small loin roast to cook or have cooked in whatever manner I pleased.

'It was the meat of a freshly killed man, who seemed to be about thirty years old – and had not been murdered.

'Neither then or at any time since have I had any serious personal qualms, either of digestion or conscience, but despite time, distance, and *locale* I feel that it would be unfair, unsporting, and ungrateful to involve and identify too closely the individual friends who made my experience possible.

'Fortunately such identification will not be necessary to establish authenticity. When a man has actually done a special thing of this sort he need very worry about whether it will be accepted as authentic. Some millions of people will sooner or later read these lines in one language or another. No matter what phrases I choose, whether I write well or awkwardly, the authenticity will take care of itself, for I propose to set down details as full, objective, and complete as if I were recounting a first experience with reindeer meat, shark meat, or any other unfamiliar meat experimented with for the first time.

'The raw meat, in appearance, was firm, slightly coarse-textured rather than smooth. In raw texture both to the eye and to the touch, it resembled good beef. In colour, however, it was slightly less red than beef. But it was reddish. It was not pinkish or greyish, like mutton or pork. Through the red lean ran fine whitish fibres, interlacing, seeming to be stringy rather than fatty, suggesting that it might be tough. The solid fat was faintly yellow, as the fat of beef and mutton is. This yellow tinge was very faint, but it was not clear white, as pork fat is.

'In smell it had what I can only describe as the familiar, characteristic smell of any good fresh meat of the larger domestic animals. I am not expert in the finest shades of odour. When various meats begin cooking there are special odours, easily distinguishable once they begin sizzling, as, for instance, beef, mutton, and pork. But in the raw state meats even so different as the three I have mentioned smell exactly alike to me, and this present meat smelled the same.

'Having at hand my portion of highly seasoned stew, prepared in the classic manner (and not yet tasted, because I was anxious to get the clearest first impression possible of the natural meat, and feared that excessive condiments would render it inconclusive), I had determined to prepare the steak and roast in the simplest manner, as nearly as possible as we prepare meat at home. The small roast was spitted, since an oven was out of the question, and after it had been cooking for a while I set about grilling the steak. I tried to do it exactly as we do at home. It took longer, but that may have been partly because of the difference between gas-flame and wood-fire.

'The cooking odours, wholly pleasant, were like those of beefsteak and roast beef, with no other special distinguishing odour. By "other distinguishing odour" I mean that if you go into a kitchen where they are cooking game or mutton or fish or chicken there is in each case something quite special, which you can distinguish with the nose alone.

'When the roast began to brown and the steak to turn blackish on the outside I cut into them, to have a look at the partially cooked interior. It had turned quite definitely paler than beef would turn. It was turning greyish, as veal or lamb would, rather than dark reddish, as a beefsteak turns. The fat was sizzling, becoming tender and yellower. Beyond what I have told there was nothing special or unusual. It was nearly done, and it looked and smelled good to eat.

'It would have been obviously stupid to go to all this trouble and then to taste too meticulously and with too much experimental nervousness only tiny morsels. I had cooked it as one would any other meat for my regular evening dinner, and I proposed to make a meal of it as one would of any other meat, with rice and a bottle of wine. That seemed to be the way to do it. I wanted to be absolutely sure of my impressions.

'I sat down to it with my bottle of wine, a bowl of rice, salt and pepper at hand. I had thought about this and planned it for a long time, and now I was going to do it. I was going to do it, furthermore – I had promised and told myself – with a completely casual, open, and objective mind. But I was soon to discover that I had bluffed and deceived myself a little in pretending so detached an attitude. It was with, or rather after, the first mouthful that I discovered there had been unconscious bravado in me, a small, bluff-hidden, unconscious dread. For my first despicable reaction – so strong that it took complete precedence over any satisfaction or any fine points of gastronomic shading – was simply a feeling of thankful and immense relief. At any rate, it was perfectly good to eat! At any rate, it had no weird, startling, or unholy special flavour. It was good to eat, and despite all the intelligent, academic detachment with which I had thought I was approaching the experience, my poor little cowardly and prejudiced, subconscious real self sighed with relief and patted itself on the back.

'I took a good big swallow of wine, a helping of rice, and thoughtfully ate half the steak. And as I ate I knew with increasing conviction and certainty exactly what it was like. It was like good, fully developed veal, not young, but not yet beef. It was very definitely like that, and it was not like any other meat I had ever tasted. It was so nearly like good, fully developed veal that I think no person with a palate of ordinary, normal sensitiveness could distinguish it from veal. It was a mild, good meat, with no other sharply defined or highly characteristic taste, such as, for instance, goat, high game, and pork have. The steak was slightly tougher than prime veal, a little stringy, but not too tough or too stringy to be agreeably edible. The roast, from which I cut and ate a central slice, was tender, and in colour, texture, smell, as well as taste, strengthened my certainty that of all the meats we habitually know veal is the one meat to which this meat is accurately comparable. As for any other special taste or odour, of a sort which would be surprising and make a person who had tasted it not knowing exclaim, "What is this?" it had absolutely none. And as for the "long pig" legend, repeated in a thousand stories and reco-pied in a hundred books, it was totally, completely false. It gives me great comfort here to be able to write thus categorically. A small helping of the stew might likewise have been veal stew, but the over-abundance of red pepper was such that it conveyed no fine shade of flavour to a white palate; so I was glad I had tried it first in the simpler ways.

If I had begun, despite my objective intentions, with a certain unconscious trepidation, I finished well enough, able after the first sensation of relief had passed to consider the meat as meat, and to be absolutely sure of the correctness of my impressions. And I felt a great satisfaction in having learned the empiric truth on a subject concerning which far too many books and pieces have been written and rewritten, filled with almost nothing but speculation, hearsay, legend, and hot air. A sense of pride also in having carried something through to its finish. And a long-standing personal curiosity satisfied at last.'

William Seabrook never satisfied another personal curiosity in quite such a bizarre manner as this taste of cannibalism. Though he continued to travel restlessly, sample every sensation to the full and wrote several more vivid travelogues during the years of the Second World War, he was already a doomed man. A mixture of exhaustion and a suggestion of insanity finally burned him out, and on the morning of 20 September 1945 with the dawn of the post-war world breaking all around him, Seabrook was found dead at this home in Rhinebeck, New York.

The 'White Cannibal of New York' – as one of the tabloid obituaries dubbed him the following day – had committed suicide. An early rumour that he had died while performing yet another bizarre secret ritual was soon scotched by the coroner. This man of a thousand thrills had died prosaically from an overdose of pills.

The Düsseldorf Monster

Peter Kurten, a debonair, middle-aged man with an admiration for Jack the Ripper, caused a reign of terror in Germany in the early thirties that caused more bloodshed and panic than even his infamous London mentor. Impeccably dressed, with a pleasant, low-pitched voice, Kurten charmed and then slaughtered a series of unsuspecting women and girls in order to satisfy his insatiable craving for human blood. He has since gone down in criminal history as one of the worst serial-killers of this century.

During the years of his crimes, Kurten carried out murder by strangulation, by stabbing and with the use of a hammer. He also attempted to kill people on several other occasions, as well as committing bestiality, torture and arson. And before he was finally caught, this debonair killer's versatility and vampire-like methods earned him the terrible reputation throughout Germany as 'The Düsseldorf Monster'.

Kurten's victims included children as well as women and young girls. He certainly killed nine people, probably twelve, and more than likely several more. Even those who were lucky enough to survive his sadistic and perverted attacks were left scarred for the rest of their lives.

Yet despite all the crimes which were laid at Peter Kurten's door, the man himself had seemed for some years to be a model of propriety. A devoted family man, he was said to love children. A conscientious worker at the factory where he was employed, he was also a keen trade unionist. Others spoke of him as a regular church-goer and devout Catholic. But how wrong those who had imagined that *this* was the real Kurten – including even his wife – were to be proved . . .

Peter Kurten was born in Mulheim in the Ruhr in 1883, the eldest child in an impoverished family of ten. His father was a malevolent drunkard who viciously ill-treated him and his hard-working mother. Displays of temper, bullying, brutality and foul-mouthed tirades were everyday events in the Kurten household. In truth, just surviving was the overriding concern of young Peter's life, and it is no surprise to learn that he had turned to crime by the time he was a teenager. His brothers and sisters also stole and pilfered, until the sudden death of their father caused the break-up of the family.

Little is known of Kurten's life thereafter until 1923 when he had moved south from Mulheim to

Düsseldorf and got married. Here it seemed he had at last been able to overcome his appalling childhood and turn his back on crime. Helped by his wife Berthe, a rather plain woman some years older than himself, he had secured a job in a local factory. He had also, though, already begun to show the signs of narcissism that would later take on much darker undertones.

There has been a great deal of discussion among historians of crime about Berthe Kurten and how a man of Peter's ego and sexual proclivities could have come to marry her. And not just marry her, but according to later reports threaten to kill her while they were courting unless she did so. He was certainly not after her money – because she was as poor as he was – nor did she seem to have any sex appeal. It may just have been her loyalty, which was given so unquestioningly, that attracted him, these historians feel, and which also unsuspectingly sustained him until the terrible facts of his secret life at last came to light.

Frau Kurten supplemented her husband's salary from the factory by taking a night job in the kitchen of a café about a mile from their modest apartment home. Each night Peter would escort her to work and then meet her again when she finished at dawn. It was quite evident all along that she knew nothing of what he did in the hours in between.

The reign of terror that was to grip Düsseldorf, just as the killings of Jack the Ripper had done over forty years earlier in London, began in February 1929 when the body of a nine-year-old child was discovered brutally murdered. The tiny corpse had not only been strangled, but there were signs that some blood had been taken from the neck by the use of a knife. An attempt had also been made to burn the body.

A few days later, a teenage girl was found at another secluded spot not far away. She had been stabbed and mutilated, too, and it appeared that blood had been sucked from her shoulder and breasts. There was evidence that she had been raped by her assailant before being killed.

Within the month a third victim was found, this time beaten to death with a hammer and her body slashed with knife-wounds. Once again there were clear signs that the killer was afflicted by a lust for blood.

All of a sudden no one in Düsseldorf felt safe to go out of doors at night. Mounted police patrols were set up to cover the area and the wildest rumours about the murderer flew around as neighbour began to suspect neighbour.

As the wave of panic in the city grew, Peter Kurten continued escorting his wife to and from her work as if nothing untoward was happening. His sartorial elegance, if anything, increased. He was never seen other than impeccably dressed: his chin closely shaved, his hands meticulously clean and his hair neatly brushed. His suits, too, were always carefully pressed and his shoes polished till they shone. Around him, too, there hung the faint odour of an expensive cologne.

Frau Kurten's fellow workers were charmed by Peter's quiet courtesy. Several sensed his appeal to the opposite sex and were curious why he should have married such a nondescript woman. None, though, had the faintest idea of what he did after strolling nonchalantly away from the café into the Düsseldorf night.

Those who suspected he was a bit of a ladies' man were certainly right. In fact, Peter had become sexually aware at a very young age and had first experienced sexual intercourse when he was twelve. But what he now wanted most from women was their blood. He had discovered that the sight and the taste of it gave his oversexed ego an amazing physical stimulus.

This lust for blood had apparently first manifested itself when he was a boy while visiting the local abattoir in Mulheim. He had stood for hours on end morbidly watching the slaughtering of animals, then, surreptitiously, and with increasing enthusiasm he had answered an inner compulsion to taste some of the dead animals' blood – sucking great globs of it with his fingers. The effect was electrifying; and once he had tasted blood, his craving grew.

With time, the appeal of animal blood began to pale and Peter's compulsion told him it was only really an unsatisfactory substitute for human blood. More than this, it was probably only the blood of women that would bring him true satisfaction.

Kurten's appearance belied all this inner turmoil. His personal fastidiousness and stylish dressing made him look younger than his years, and certainly did not suggest to any woman whom he engaged in conversation that here was someone who had grown up under the constant threat of a beating and harboured an unholy desire to suck blood.

Even when the attacks on women were the talk of everyone in Düsseldorf, Berthe Kurten still had no reason to think she was married to a monster. Each day she shopped in the neighbourhood as usual and at night Peter continued to escort her to and from work. Life in their flat was a haven of tranquillity while all around them the nerves and tempers of their neighbours grew more frayed as one report of a brutal killing was soon followed by another. The police seemed helpless to stop the murderer who slunk in and out of the shadows with ease. If he was going to be caught, people whispered in their homes, on street corners and at work, it would be when he made a mistake. And so it proved.

On the night of 14 May 1930 Peter Kurten got into conversation with a young woman who had just travelled to the city from Cologne to take up a new job. Charmed by his politeness and his offer of accommodation – so the subsequent trial proceedings revealed – she went willingly with him to some lodgings he had rented in the Mettmanner-strasse. There he attempted unsuccessfully to rape her.

In the past when his advances had been rejected, Peter Kurten had reacted with violence and sadism. But this time for some strange reason he did not. Instead, when the girl begged him to let her go and pleaded that she did not know the city well enough to tell anyone where he had taken her, he agreed. Equally strangely, and good as her word, the girl did not report the incident – although she did mention it in a letter written to a friend a few days later.

In all probability still affected by her ordeal, the girl addressed the letter incorrectly and a few days later it ended up in the Düsseldorf dead-letter file. There it was opened by a clerk in order that it could be re-addressed and returned to the sender. However, human curiosity being what it is, the man could not help glancing down at the letter and at once realised the significance of the writer's remarks about her attack.

The alert clerk duly informed the police, and once the girl had been located, she directed them at once to the address in the Mettmannerstrasse. At last the officers of the law felt they were on the trail of the Vampire of Düsseldorf.

That same night Peter Kurten escorted his wife to the café as usual and then set off to his secret lodgings. As he turned into the street he saw a policeman stationed outside the building. He did not need a second look to realise the game was up. The owner of the flat did not know his real name, but he knew what he looked like and there could not be too many quietly-spoken, debonair men in the city who would have no alibi whatsoever for the hours between nightfall and dawn on *any* day. Other wives would know where their husbands were each night – Frau Kurten, on the other hand, had no idea because she was always at work.

When Peter met her in the half-light of the following morning he was ready to confess everything.

'Listen,' he said, taking both her hands in his. 'I want you to be the first to know that I have been responsible for everything that has been happening here in Düsseldorf. I am the Düsseldorf murderer.'

Berthe Kurten looked at her husband totally uncomprehendingly.

'No, Peter,' she said, haltingly. 'You are a good man. I know you chase girls. But they chase you, too. You could not kill anyone.'

'But I did. The children, too.'

'Those innocent children!' her voice then became a muffled scream. 'Oh, God, what made you do it? Peter, what made you do it?'

An agonised silence fell between the couple before Peter Kurten spoke again.

'Something – I can't describe it – something happens to me,' he stuttered. 'It's the blood. Their blood. I have to have it. To taste it. To drink it. That's all.'

For the next hour Peter Kurten tried to convince his wife that she must go and report him to the police. There was a substantial reward out for his capture, he said, and if she was to claim it she would be secure after he was gone. The longer he argued, however, the more adamant she became. She would not report him, she said; he had to give himself up. Finally, reluctantly, they parted company for the last time. When Frau Kurten reached her front door half an hour later she found the police were already waiting.

The trial of Peter Kurten opened in Düsseldorf in April 1931. He was tried with a total of nine murders to which his counsel entered a plea of insanity. He sat stony-faced and unmoving as the prosecutor reeled off the catalogue of brutal murders, sadism and perversions with which he was charged. They amounted to as grim a list of crimes as any presented in legal history.

The stories of how he had lulled his victims with his impeccable manners and soothing voice before so callously butchering them brought tears to the eyes of many of the packed courtroom as well as the occasional cries of horror and revulsion. Here was a man to whom blood was an obsession and whose craving for it knew no bounds. He seemed to some listeners worse even than a vampire. And not once did he show so much as a glimmer of remorse.

A noted German psychiatrist, Professor Karl Berg, was also called to give evidence and told the court that from his observations of Kurten he believed him to be a man who found fulfilment in acts of mutilation. He was stimulated at the sight of blood and the humiliation of his victims. Indeed, Berg believed that Kurten gained a sense of achievement in the very act of killing.

At the end of the trial, Kurten was found guilty on all nine counts of murder and sentenced to death. He was ordered to be executed by the guillotine at Klingelputz Prison in Cologne on 2 July 1931. He continued to remain cool and detached to the end, his fascination with blood undiminished to the very last moment of his life.

According to records at the Klingelputz Prison, just before his execution Peter Kurten ate a substantial meal and, for his final request, was even allowed a second helping. Then he stood up and, fastidious as ever, carefully wiped his mouth before turning to the executioner, who had silently entered the room to take him away. The last words he was ever heard to speak made even that man, who was hardened to death, shudder and appreciate just why the 'Monster of Düsseldorf' would become known as such a unique figure among mass-murderers.

'Shall I hear, if only for a moment, my own blood gush and spout into the basket as I die?' he asked with just the hint of a smile across his immaculate features. 'That would be the most exquisite, intense pleasure of all.'

The Vampire Murderer

The vampire has become one of the twentieth century's most popular figure in horror stories and films. Although the tradition of the undead creature able to rise from its grave and sustain its existence by drinking the blood of the living has been known for centuries, there are few authenticated accounts of blood-drinking ghouls in the British Isles.

One exception to this is John George Haigh, whom the *Daily Mirror* named as 'The Vampire Murderer' in 1949 for his series of brutal murders in which he used sulphuric acid to destroy the bodies of his victims after he had drunk their still-warm blood. The names of few murderers have come to be more reviled or are more likely to send a shiver up the spine than that of this man, who has also gone down in criminal history as the perpetrator of what are known as 'The Acid Bath Murders'.

The roots of Haigh's obsession with blood which led him into a life of crime were said to have been sown in his childhood, which was extremely strict and repressive. He was born in Yorkshire in 1909, the son of a colliery foreman. Both his parents belonged to the Plymouth Brethren, and from his childhood they had instructed him that all organised pleasure was 'sinful', while newspapers of any kind were never to be allowed into the home because of their immoral attitudes.

Young John George Haigh was, however, an extremely bright child, and delighted his parents by winning a scholarship to Wakefield Grammar School. He also had a beautiful singing voice and this won him an additional choral scholarship which involved singing at high church services in Wakefield Cathedral.

Those experts who have studied Haigh's life believe that he found the pomp and circumstance of the Church of England ceremonial such a contrast to the starkness of the Plymouth Brethren rituals that they soon prompted the most voluptuous and vivid dreams in his young mind. Indeed, Haigh later stated that his teenage years and been 'full of dream visions of forests that spouted blood' and it was these, he said, that had later induced him to murder. Furthermore, it was these dreams of blood that had excited vampirish longings in him.

Although his sheltered childhood had prevented Haigh from ever reading any books about vampires, in his nightmares he saw himself drinking from containers of fresh blood and even tasting human flesh from which the blood flowed. The songs he sang as a chorister also filled his imagination with visions of suffering and pain that seemed somehow enjoyable to both those who were enduring the torture and those inflicting it. Undoubtedly, the character of the mass-murderer was formed in those years.

Apart from his intelligence, Haigh was also blessed with dark good looks. He always dressed smartly, wore a neatly-trimmed moustache and invariably kept his hair well groomed and slicked back from his high forehead. His eyes, too, could as easily sparkle with mischief as menace.

But though he was a natural charmer with a way with women, Haigh was also a wastrel and the evidence shows that he had already begun to dabble in petty crime when the first significant event of his life occurred: his marriage to Beatrice Hamer in 1934. In fact, little is known of the girl – or about the couple's marriage – beyond the fact that they parted soon after Haigh had served the first of several prison sentences for fraud in the November of that same year.

Throughout much of the thirties, John George Haigh appears to have regularly come to the attention of the authorities for committing theft and fraud of one kind or another – though rarely with much success and usually ending with him in prison. Still, he continued this feckless career of crime during the early years of the Second World War and was next heard of in 1943 living in a flat, number 404, at the Onslow Court Hotel in South Kensington.

The Onslow Court was a highly respectable residence, occupied mainly by professional and retired people. Here Haigh apparently used all his charm to become accepted by the other occupants. If at times he seemed a little too cocksure and no one was quite certain what his occupation was – he used to side-step such questions with a vague reference to being 'an engineer' – Haigh's pleasant manner soon silenced any doubts.

Unbeknownst to his fellow residents, the handsome former choirboy continued to earn his living by various kinds of petty fraud, until the fateful day he became friendly with a sixty-nine-year-old Olive Durand-Deacon. This wealthy widow who lived on the same floor as Haigh confided in him her ideas of marketing cosmetic fingernails. Never slow to spot a opportunity for a con, Haigh invited her to visit what he called his 'factory' in Sussex which might be just what she needed to set up her business. In fact it was no more than a store-room to some premises to which he had access in Leopold Road, Crawley – but nevertheless on 18 February he drove the unsuspecting widow there from Kensington.

According to the subsequent evidence given in court when Haigh came to trial, he had been to the store-room earlier and laid his plans. In the room were an empty forty-gallon drum, a large quantity of sulphuric acid, a pair of rubber gloves and an apron. As soon as Mrs Durand-Deacon walked through the unprepossessing store-room door her fate was sealed.

Without a moment's hesitation, Haigh cold-bloodedly shot the widow through the back of the neck. Then, it was alleged, he licked lasciviously at the blood running down her shoulders as she lay on the floor. Having satisfied this craving, he stripped the old woman's body of its valuables and tipped the corpse into the empty drum. Onto this he poured the sulphuric acid and then, unobserved still, left the premises. With the stolen jewellery which he took to a local pawn shop he was able to satisfy his equally desperate need for cash.

Between 21 and 28 February, Haigh returned to the store-room in Crawley several times to ensure that his victim's body was being satisfactorily destroyed in the acid. On each occasion he topped up the level, and when he finally believed all traces of Mrs Durand-Deacon had gone he tipped the remaining sludge out into the yard.

In the interim, the charmer of Onslow Court had also talked one of the other residents into going to Chelsea Police Station to report Mrs Durand-Deacon's 'disappearance'. Because their friendship was known to everyone in the hotel, he said he had arranged to meet her at the Army and Navy Stores in Victoria, but she had failed to arrive.

However, at the police station an alert policewoman, Sergeant Lambourne, instinctively distrusted Haigh's glibness about the alleged disappearance and, after he had left, decided to check if the man had any kind of record. The files soon disclosed his long history of fraud and theft – and when the police began checking up on Haigh and discovered that he had recently been settling some long-standing debts, there seemed good reason to suspect he might be implicated in Mrs Durand-Deacon's mysterious disappearance.

Sooner than expected, the trail led the police to the store-room in Leopold Road where traces of blood were found on the walls and a .38 Webley was discovered in a hat-box. There were also clear signs that the weapon had been fired recently.

On 28 February, Haigh was summarily arrested and taken to Chelsea Police Station. In the hours which followed be began to admit to a horrendous catalogue of murders as well as confessing his predilection for vampirism.

Initially, however, Haigh showed little sign of emotion when told that his store-room at Crawley had been found and searched. But when Detective-Inspector Albert Webb, who was leading the enquiries, mentioned the spots of blood on the walls, the suspect's reaction was both sudden and unexpected. It was almost as if the demons of his childhood dreams had come back to haunt him once again.

'Mrs Durand-Deacon no longer exists,' he was

quoted as shouting at his questioner. 'I've destroyed her with acid. You can't prove murder without a body!'

Haigh then startled the policeman even more by asking what the chances were of getting out of Broadmoor – surely one of the most extraordinary remarks ever made by a suspect, guilty or otherwise.

There was though, an even greater surprise in store for Detective-Inspector Webb when he charged Haigh with the murder of Mrs Durand-Deacon. A grin seemed to spread across the man's even features, and then he confessed to having killed at least seven other victims. He had drunk their blood, too, he said, and also disposed of their bodies in baths of acid.

In his subsequent statement, Haigh claimed that he had been motivated by the same lust that had possessed him from childhood. He felt the need to drink the blood of each of his victims, and could still remember the warm, sticky sensation it had on his lips and in his mouth.

The understandably horrified police were then left to assemble the evidence of these other killings. Starting in Haigh's flat in the Onslow Court Hotel, their hunt was made easier by the discovery of a number of documents relating to the sale of valuable items of property and jewellery which the killer had kept and which made it easier to link his name to that of his victims.

There had been three members of a family

named McSwann – a father, mother and son – then the Hendersons, a doctor and his wife. Donald McSwann had apparently been the first to die in September 1944, and he was followed by his parents in July of the next year. Haigh met the Hendersons in 1947 and thereafter set out to systematically swindle them before luring both to his 'factory' and killing and disposing of them in the same manner he had used for Mrs Durand-Deacon. From these deaths and the forgeries he initiated in the names of his victims, Haigh was believed to have netted at least £8,000 as well as property and other items of value.

During the hours that he spent making his statement – and throughout which he repeatedly referred to his partiality for drinking the blood of his victims – Haigh also claimed he had murdered another couple he only remembered as Max and Mary. However, police enquiries failed to establish whether these two had ever existed or were just a figment of the killer's imagination. Certainly no trace of them was ever found.

There were, however, traces of Mrs Durand-Deacon's body brought to light by the police forensic investigation at Leopold Road to dumbfound Haigh's claim that she no longer existed. By painstakingly sifting through the nauseating sludge in the yard, the forensic team found a number of human remains. Apart from twenty-eight pounds of body fat, the investigators discovered bits of a pelvis, an ankle, a heel-bone, some gall-stones and part of a pair of false teeth. These grisly relics, along with a hairpin, some cosmetic containers and a red plastic handbag had clearly belonged to a woman. It was the false teeth which proved the most conclusive piece of evidence when they were identified by Mrs Durand-Deacon's dentist.

The details of these discoveries – as well as the list of Haigh's victims – made the subsequent trial a sensation even before it opened. The hints of blood-drinking and vampirism made it even more of a tabloid newspaper's dream, and the *Daily Mirror*, then the biggest-selling popular newspaper in Britain, unwisely overstepped the mark in its enthusiasm for a good story before the trial by referring to Haigh as a vampire.

The story was a clear example of contempt of court and not surprisingly landed the *Mirror* itself in court. Though endeavouring to justify its statement on the grounds that Haigh had never denied his blood-drinking, the paper was still fined £10,000 and the editor Silvester Bolam was given a three-month jail sentence.

The trial of the 'Vampire Murderer' opened at Lewes Assizes, Sussex on 18 July 1949 before Mr Justice Humphreys. Sir Hartley Shawcross, KC, prosecuted the case for the Crown, with Sir David Maxwell Fyfe, KC, appearing for the defence and offering a plea of insanity on behalf of Haigh.

A crucial witness was Dr Henry Yellowlees, a psychiatrist, who was cross-examined about Haigh's claims of vampirism. He said that he agreed with the theory that the defendant had become a paranoiac owing to the stifling environment in which he had grown up.

'I believe it is pretty certain that Haigh drank the blood of his victims,' Dr Yellowlees stated, adding the further startling information that Haigh had been observed drinking his own urine while in custody at Brixton Prison.

The case, with its elements of corpses being disposed of in acid baths and a killer who lapped the warm blood of his victims, provided some of the most fulsome coverage and biggest headlines ever seen in the British press of the time. It is also said to have been the spark which prompted a new wave of interest in vampirism and resulted in several new books and films.

The jury at Lewes, however, were singularly unmoved by the plea of insanity and took less than a quarter of an hour to deliver a verdict of guilty. Three weeks later, on 10 August, John George Haigh was executed at Wandsworth Prison. He was only thirty-nine years old, but had already assured himself a unique 'double' in British criminal history as well as in the annals of vampirism.

The Psycho-Killer

Alfred Hitchcock's movie, *Psycho* (1960), about the isolated motel killer Norman Bates who has a mother-fixation which takes control of his life, has been called 'one of the most famous horror movies of all time'. A quarter of a century later, Tobe Hooper's grisly *Texas Chainsaw Massacre*, which features a backwoods serial-killer, has also been described as 'probably the most terrifying slasher movie ever made'. Both films were, though, according to their authors, inspired by the same true story – that of an American farmer named Ed Gein who became a murdering ghoul and cannibal, and whose exploits were actually far more ghastly than anything shown in either of the classic movies.

The revelations in 1957 about what had been going on behind the curtains of Ed Gein's clapboard farmhouse where he lived alone in Plainfield, Wisconsin, not only shocked the whole of America but ultimately gave the world a new word:

'psycho'. On the surface, Ed had appeared a middle-aged farmer who had been denied a normal interest in women by his overbearing mother and as a result had become a rather pathetic loner. But when policemen investigating the disappearance of a local store-owner burst into his home they found before their eyes the gruesome evidence that Gein was actually a mass-killer and cannibal: a man not merely content to eat his victims' flesh, but actually to wear the skin from their corpses draped over his own body. Of all the serial-killers of the twentieth century he has been among the worst – and certainly the most bizarre.

Edward Gein was born on 27 August 1906, the second son of Augusta and George Gein, the owners of a family grocery store in La Crosse, Wisconsin. Ed and his older brother Henry enjoyed largely uneventful childhoods, though both were rigidly governed by their domineering mother.

A significant event in young Ed's life occurred when he disobeyed a strict rule of his mother's that he was never to enter the little slaughter house behind the grocery store where she and her husband prepared their own meat for sale. When, out of curiosity, he finally decided to defy this exhortation, he opened the door to find both his parents in ankle-length leather aprons, splattered with blood from the pig carcass, hanging upside-down from the ceiling, which they were carving up. But it was the image of his mother actually pulling the flesh from the animal that was to remain most vividly with the young child for the rest of his life.

When Ed was eight, the family moved to a 195-acre farm in Plainfield which they worked with reasonable success until the sudden death of George Gein in April 1940. The younger son was now thirty-four, and though generally liked by people in the local community, he was thought to be 'a bit strange' because of his unwholesome attachment to his mother. This reputation for 'strangeness' was not helped by the fact he had a drooping left eyelid and a habit of laughing at the most inappropriate times.

After her husband's death, Augusta Gein kept both of her sons busy on the farm as refused to let them go courting local girls and most of their contemporaries were doing. In May 1944, a second tragedy hit the Gein family when a fire which had been started by the two brothers to clear some grassland got out of control and claimed the life of Henry Gein.

Just over a year later, in December 1945, Augusta Gein herself died after a series of strokes. Her only surviving son was devastated by this latest blow – believing that it was the hard life on the farm and the moral degeneracy of the world in general that had lead to his mother's death. Within a matter of days he had begun turning in on himself: he sealed off his mother's room and the parlour just as she had left them and thereafter occupied only the rear part of the house.

In the months and years which followed, Ed Gein allowed the farm to fall into neglect while he started his own descent into the madness and perversion which would ultimately lead to murder. He also took to reading books about the human body, and developed a special fascination with the female anatomy. When this interest turned inexorably into an obsession, he decided to pursue it at first hand by secretly digging up corpses from two of the local graveyards.

To the people of Plainfield, Ed still seemed no more eccentric than he had been all his life. He did the occasional odd jobs and was even seen from time to time trying rather awkwardly to get two middle-aged women to go dancing or to the films with him. Both of these women were said later to have been curiously like Ed's mother in appearance – but neither took him up on his offer.

During the years from 1947 to 1958, life in Plainfield continued much as normal, although a number of women and a couple of young girls did go missing under puzzling circumstances. The first of these was an eight-year-old babysitter, Georgia Weckler, who was never seen again after leaving for her home on 1 May 1947. In October 1953, another babysitter, fifteen-year-old Evelyn Hartly, also disappeared from the house where she was sitting for the evening. In her case, a trail of blood indicated that at best she had been abducted, and at worst murdered. But neither her body nor that of little Georgia were ever found.

The subsequent disappearance of an older woman, Mary Hogan, in 1954, was the first to alert the local community that a killer might be on the loose. Then when a series of curious occurrences were followed by another middle-aged lady, Bernice Worden, going missing under not dissimilar circumstances in November 1957, the people of Plainfield could no longer have any doubts.

Throughout this time, strange stories had also begun to be whispered about Ed Gein – though no one connected them with the disappearances. It was said that after leasing off some of his fields to neighbouring farmers in order to pay his bills, he had even tried to sell the property. But he was reluctant to let anyone into the farmhouse to view, and would never show any prospective buyer beyond the parlour and his mother's bedroom – both still as pristine as the day she had died.

Local children also fuelled the gossip with stories of being shown shrunken heads by Ed which he said he had bought by mail order. Another rumour claimed the decaying farmhouse was now haunted and that a naked woman with flowing hair had been seen cavorting there on a number of evenings by the light of the moon.

It was, though, the evidence of two eye-witnesses who had seen Ed Gein going into Bernice Worden's grocery store in Plainfield shortly before her disappearance on Saturday, 16 November 1957, that first really pointed the finger of suspicion at the little farmer and made the local sheriff Art Schley decide to question him. Traces of bloodstains in the store and the fact that a delivery truck was missing made the lawman fear the worst.

Extraordinarily, when Ed Gein was confronted by the sheriff leaving the home of a neighbour with whom he had just had dinner, he damned himself out of his own mouth. If they were looking for Mrs Worden's killer and thought it might be him, he said, then he had been framed.

But neither Sheriff Schley or his deputies had mentioned Mrs Worden – let alone suggested she might be dead.

At eight p.m. that night, as the questioning of Ed Gein began in the Plainfield police headquarters, Schley and several other lawmen entered his farmhouse armed only with torches. What met their horrified eyes was like a vision from hell, a nightmare of such ghastly proportions that none of the men could quite believe what they were seeing.

Hanging upside-down from the ceiling of the kitchen was the body of Bernice Worden. She was naked and had been slit open from her stomach to her collarbone. The corpse had also been disembowelled and decapitated. It was as if Ed Gein had precisely re-enacted the terrible scene of his mother with the pig which had so scarred his childhood memories.

Fighting back their nausea, the lawmen looked around the kitchen. On a table, wrapped in plastic, were Bernice Worden's heart and entrails. Beside these grisly relics was the top half of a skull that had evidently been used as a food bowl. The kitchen chairs were also found to be woven with strips of human skin.

All around was the detritus of a solitary old man's life: unwashed dishes, fading newspapers and magazines, and piles of dirty clothes. The place reeked from the filth and accumulation of rubbish. In the other rooms – except Ed's mother's bedroom and the parlour – still more terrible evidence of his ghoulish life came to light.

In Ed's bedroom, the sheriff and his men found two skulls impaled on the posts of the bed. A lampshade covered with human skin stood on a table beside this, along with a knife with a handle made from what proved to be a human bone.

Then came the foullest horrors of all in the bedroom cupboard.

Opening the doors, Sheriff Schley saw what he at first imagined to be a pair of leggings and a woman's swimming costume. In fact the leggings had been cut from human skin, and the 'costume' was the complete front part of a female torso which had been dried and had strings attached to it so that it could be worn. A shoebox on the floor was found to contain eight dried vulvas – several with string attached to them – all apparently intended to be worn. One was even curiously painted in silver.

Also brought to light in that cupboard of death was the flesh from four faces which had been stuffed with paper and were clearly intended to be worn as masks. A couple of these had been oiled to retain their softness, while the other pair had been allowed to go hard. All had lipstick applied to the lips. One lawman, on the point of being physically ill, identified one of the 'masks' as the face of Mary Hogan, the woman who had disappeared in 1954, and whom he had known.

Still the horrors kept appearing in the torch-light's glare. Another box was found which contained four noses, several sets of lips and various other parts from human heads. In several more buckets, jars, plastic containers and sacks the investigators discovered an assortment of bones, flesh, breasts, nipples and bits of genitalia from an uncountable number of bodies.

The last discovery that terrible night was Bernice Worden's head. It had been hidden under a blanket and had two bent nails already fixed to the ears joined by a length of twine so that this, the very latest grisly souvenir of Ed Gein's madness, was ready to be hung up . . .

'The Plainfield Butcher' – as Ed Gein would later be named by the press of America – confessed haltingly to his crimes. He could account for most of the bodies, he said, by the fact that he had made over forty visits to the Plainfield and Springfield cemeteries between 1947 and 1954 to rob graves. Eventually, he accounted for a total of twelve bodies, though the evidence of the remains found in the farmhouse made the more likely total to be at least fifteen. Unfortunately, any chance of ever finalising the number of corpses was lost forever early the following year on 30 March 1958 when a mysterious fire burned the property to the ground. Rumour has suggested that it was the handiwork of some local people who regarded the farmhouse as a place of unmitigated evil – though this, too, has never been proved.

On 6 January, 1958, Ed Gein was found unfit to stand trial and committed for life to the Wisconsin Central State Hospital for the criminally insane. His confession, which was read at the hearing, revealed a man lost in obsessions of necrophilia and cannibalism. And also a man who seemed to show no remorse for the terrible outrages he had committed.

In his statement, Ed was quite open about his purpose for the female parts that had been found in his home. They were to be worn. And in making this confession, he laid to rest the story of the haunting at the farm house.

On warm, moonlit nights, he explained, he used to strip naked and strap on the preserved torso, breasts and leggings. Then he would tie a vagina over his penis and choose one of the face masks to put over his head. Thus horrifyingly attired, he would go out into the farmyard and dance to his heart's content.

Gein confessed that he had made a detailed study of cannibalism, and when answering the questions which were put to him about how he had dismembered the corpses, showed what his interrogators described as 'a considerable knowledge of the subject'. He found the taste of flesh made him feel 'a bit sick', he said, but could not resist the sensation of intimate parts of female flesh on his skin.

He had tasted the blood of several of his victims, he added.

All of these experiences gave him an intense feeling of gratification, Gein said. And he had especially chosen a number of the corpses he stole from graveyards – as well as at least two of the women he killed – because of their physical resemblance to 'my saintly mother'. A suggestion that he actually had sexual intercourse with some of these bodies was never resolved conclusively, although during one period of interrogation he told a psychiatrist from the Central State Hospital that he never did so because the corpses 'smelled too bad'.

Ed Gein spent the rest of his life in custody and eventually died on 26 July 1984 of respiratory failure. His body was taken back with a minimum of fuss to the Plainfield Cemetery that he had so often violated, and there laid to rest beside that of his beloved mother.

The fame of 'the Plainfield Butcher' was only just beginning, however. Apart from the two movies, his crimes have also been retold in a number of books of non-fiction as well as several novels and movies. In the ranks of the flesh-eaters he is unique, too, as the man who got inside the skins of his victims and was for a time almost literally . . . *them*.

The Cannibal of the Bois de Boulogne

There is certainly no more bizarre story in the annals of modern cannibalism than that of the Japanese student Issei Sagawa who killed and ate a fellow student while living in Paris, and now, freed from a psychiatric institution, is regarded as a celebrity in his native country. Sagawa never denied his terrible act of eating human flesh and after just four years in mental institutions, he was controversially released and has since become a familiar figure in Japan as a film actor and – of all things – the food critic of a magazine named *Spa*. He is known nationwide as the cannibal who got away with murder.

Japan has, in fact, a tradition of flesh-eating which dates back to the days of the Samurai warriors. Then a victorious member of this military caste would quite often drink the blood of any enemy he had killed in combat. Sometimes a Samurai would even eat the heart of a dead man as a sign of his complete victory.

The best known cases of Japanese cannibalism, however, date from the Second World War when the country's soldiers occupied many of the Pacific islands during their fight against the Allied Forces. Occasionally these men came into contact with the native tribesmen who were still following the old tradition and for years there were stories that some had actually shared in the meals of human flesh.

It was not, though, until some time after the war was over that concrete evidence came to light which pointed to a number of the Rising Sun's soldiers having deliberately turned to cannibalism when their supplies of food ran out. According to Toshiyuki Tanabe, an academic from Western Japan who investigated the stories, there are documents to prove that at least a hundred cases of cannibalism occurred amongst the Japanese soldiers who were abandoned in New Guinea at the end of the hostilities. Tanabe's evidence formed the basis of a controversial film, *The Emperor's Naked Army Marches On*, which was shown in Australia in 1987.

The case of Issei Sagawa, however, came to light some six years earlier in Paris in June 1981 – and in the most bizarre fashion.

Early on the morning of 16 June, walkers in the Bois de Boulogne, that vast park of over 2,000 acres which is bisected by wide, shaded roads leading to ornamental lakes, flower gardens, cafés and restaurants – not to mention the two famous racecourses of Longchamp and Auteil – were surprised to see a small, rather insignificant-looking young Japanese man wheeling through the trees a porter's barrow on which rested two large suitcases. During the French Revolution, the Bois had become a refuge for the destitute and the pursued, and there was something odd about this man's behaviour that made those who saw him suspect he might be in the same category. Indeed, one of the walkers decided to call the gendarmes when it became apparent that the little Japanese seemed to be trying to find somewhere to hide the suitcases.

A police patrol car was on the scene in minutes. But the two gendarmes who emerged were unable to find any trace of the man who had been described to them as small and thin, 'like an overgrown child'. He had dumped the cases in the bushes and fled, it seemed.

The two officers glanced at the pair of abandoned bags and shrugged their shoulders. Although both of the cases were obviously new, it seemed as if they had been called out to just another litter lout. In fact, they were about to return to their car and call in when one of the men noticed the unmistakable signs of blood seeping from the lid of one of the cases. He turned the bag on to its side and then gently prised up the lid. What he saw inside nearly turned his stomach over.

For crushed into the suitcase were several parts

of a human body. Bits of flesh, some long strands of dark hair and a number of bones. There was no mistaking, either, that they were female. When, at last, the two policemen had recovered their composure enough to open the second suitcase, they found that it, too, contained further parts of a corpse.

As soon as the horrific details of the discovery in the park had been relayed to police headquarters, a massive man-hunt across Paris was set into operation. So thorough was it that within a matter of hours the distinctive little Japanese had been tracked down – thanks mainly to the taxi driver who had driven him to the park and remembered him struggling with the two pieces of luggage.

And so five hours after the events in the Bois de Boulogne, another party of two detectives and some gendarmes were knocking at the door of a bedsit occupied by a Japanese student who had been named as Issei Sagawa. He was said to be a student at the Sorbonne and had been living there since the previous year.

The small, shy and bespectacled figure who thereupon opened the door showed no surprise at his visitors and made no attempt to deny them entry to the apartment.

Inside, the policemen soon found all the evidence they needed to connect the occupier with the grisly find in the park. There were bloodstains on one of the walls and evidence that a dead body had been moved about. More horrifying still, inside the student's refrigerator the policemen found several slices of human flesh on a plate.

Without any evident signs of emotion, Sagawa looked directly at the policemen as their eyes sought for some kind of explanation for the horror they were seeing.

'For a long time I have had a strange desire to eat a young girl,' he finally said in a quiet, matter-of-fact voice. 'Those are pieces of her flesh that I was keeping to eat later. The rest I took to the Bois de Boulogne in the suitcases.'

The 'Cannibal of the Bois de Boulogne' – as Sagawa was to be named by the French press once the story broke that evening – was hurried off for interrogation. For hour after hour he talked about himself – and the girl he had murdered and then partly eaten . . .

Issei Sagawa was thirty-one years old, the son of a millionaire Japanese businessman who had paid for him to come to Paris. He was an adored and dutiful son, who apparently spent hours each week writing long letters to his parents all about his life in Paris. At the Sorbonne, he was known by his professors as being of 'outstanding intelligence'.

The plan for Issei Sagawa had been that after completing his doctorate on the French literary influences on the Japanese Nobel prize-winning poet, Yasunari Kawabata, he would return home to start a job in his father's company. During his stay in Paris, Sagawa had also been furthering his interest in English literature – making a special study of Shakespeare's *Macbeth*.

During the course of their lengthy interrogation, the Paris police came to realise that the little Japanese had a huge ego matched to a terrific inferiority complex. He believed himself to be intellectually superior to everyone else and so felt he was not bound by normal laws of behaviour and morality. In contrast, he thought himself to be physically ugly and, unable to form relationships with any of the women he approached, turned instead to prostitutes to satisfy his sexual needs.

During his time at the Sorbonne surrounded by beautiful young women, Issei became increasingly lonely and more and more isolated. Not only did these women find his uncertain attempts at conversation embarrassing, but even the other Japanese students studying at the University found his manner arrogant and did their best to avoid his company.

Then, sometime in the winter of 1980, Sagawa met a strikingly beautiful young Dutch student named Renee Hartevelt. She was twenty-five and had won a scholarship to study French at the Sorbonne. Naturally outgoing and vivacious, she was popular with all the students. She even had a kind word for Issei, writing in one of her letters home to her parents that she had taken pity on 'this funny little Japanese guy, whom nobody else will talk to'.

Issei was captivated by Renee's beauty and her friendliness. He began to write her love letters, but when he attempted actual advances she politely but firmly rejected him. Indeed, it was only because of feeling sorry for him that she finally accepted one of his persistent entreaties to have tea with him and help him with some translation. That kind-hearted gesture was to cost Renee her life and write a new chapter in the history of cannibalism.

Unbeknownst to anyone outside of his family, Issei Sagawa was already the owner of a .22 rifle. He had bought it, he told his mother in one of his long, rambling letters, because 'Paris is so unsafe'.

Quite what happened when Renee Hartevelt entered Sagawa's flat to take tea on that fateful evening of 15 June 1981 will never be precisely known. The little Japanese claimed later that he had proposed marriage to the girl and she had laughed as if it was a joke. He had even begged her to have sex with him. This, too, she had rejected and, then, finally, she said she had to leave.

At this moment, Issei told the police, he had reached down for his rifle and shot Renee in the back of the head. Looking down at her spread-eagled body, he realised he had the chance to satisfy his deep-seated desire to taste human flesh. And so, as darkness fell around the flat, he set about dismembering the body. Boasting later of how he had butchered the girl's flesh and

223

bones, he said that he had also taken thirty colour pictures of the whole gruesome process. He then feasted on several pieces of flesh before putting further parts into his fridge. Finally, he had stuffed the remains into the two new suitcases he was going to use for his return to Japan.

Before attempting to hide the cases, Issei had one other task to perform, it was later revealed. He sat down amidst the bloodstained scene of his butchery and carefully wrapped up a present to send off for his mother's birthday. A small woolly cat.

The effect of the news of Renee Hartevelt's murder and cannibalisation on the members of her family in Amsterdam can only be imagined. It was all the more dreadful for her mother who had suffered an earlier tragedy at the hands of the Japanese. In 1941, she and her former husband, a pilot in the Dutch Indies Air Force, had been living in Indonesia when it was invaded by the Japanese. For the next three years she had struggled to stay alive in a brutal concentration camp, before finally being released. She returned to Holland in 1947 never expecting to encounter a Japanese again.

The subsequent court appearance of Issei Sagawa in July 1981 attracted enormous interest in both France and Japan. Talking beforehand to a Japanese writer, the little student showed no remorse for what he had done.

'If I am freed, I will eat another woman.' he reportedly told the journalist. 'Renee was very appetising.'

Outraged French public opinion demanded that Sagawa should be punished with exceptional severity. It was even argued in some quarters that he should be handed over to the Japanese authorities for trial and sentencing as capital punishment no longer existed in France and he might well escape with a verdict that was too lenient. As it was, with the help of disputed medical evidence which allegedly showed a faint scarring of brain tissue from a bout of encephalitis which he had suffered in childhood, Issei Sagawa was declared insane and instead committed to a French mental institution.

There the 'Cannibal of the Bois de Boulogne' remained until 1984 when, under an agreement between France and Japan, he was transferred to a hospital in Japan. Back home, further pressure was exerted on the authorities by the wealthy Sagawa family and this resulted in their son's controversial release after he had been in psychiatric institutions in the two countries for just four years.

In the decade since his release, Issei Sagawa has become a cult figure in Japan, although in France the debate has continued about the real motivations of this modern cannibal. The answers that have been proposed by various experts are many and varied. One psychologist, for example, has suggested that Sagawa was simply attempting to escape from his isolation; while a leading criminologist believes it could have been a literal interpretation, in psychotic terms, of the lover's expression, 'You look so good I could eat you'. Another psychiatrist who examined Sagawa during his term in the French mental institution gave support to this theory, commenting grimly: 'Don't forget, the adjective tender has its origin in the butcher's shop.'

This is one story of cannibalism in the twentieth century which will undoubtedly continue to attract interest and excite controversy for years to come.

Tales of Two-Legged Mutton

China is without doubt the nation where cannibalism has flourished for the longest period of
time and where it is still being reported on a
considerable scale even today at the dawn of
the twenty-first century. It is a nation where the
eating of animal flesh – from dogs and cats to the
'delicacies' of guinea pig and raccoon – is
commonplace, and where stories of man eating
man emerge with gruesome regularity.
Throughout the world's most populous nation,
human flesh is known euphemistically as 'Two-
Legged Mutton'.

In the last months of 1992 when I first began
researching this book, the Chinese writer Zheng Yi,
who was listed as one of the country's ten most
wanted 'counter-revolutionary criminals' dramatically escaped from the country and fled through
Hong Kong to find sanctuary in the United States.
There he produced documents which revealed a

horrifying picture of cannibalism in his homeland which was far and away more widespread than anyone in the West had ever suspected.

Zheng Yi, who is forty-six years old, a bright-eyed and dynamic figure with a vision of freedom in China which is very different from that of the Communist hierarchy, was one of the leaders of the famous 1989 uprising. After the terrible events in Tienanmen Square in Beijing and the brutal suppression of the young students, Zheng was forced into hiding, where he continued to observe what was going on, record the stories of political abuse which were relayed to him, and then finally made a dash for freedom clutching his valuable dossier of official documents: irrefutable proof of the horror story he unveiled in New York in January 1993.

Calmly, Zheng described how hundreds of political prisoners had been killed and then eaten by Red Guards during the Cultural Revolution of the late sixties. Brandishing the documents he had brought out of China, he said that thousands of Communists had taken part in this cannibalism to 'prove their political purity and enthusiasm'.

Zheng said that although Chairman Mao had undoubtedly wanted a lot of those who opposed the regime to be killed, he had never gone so far as to suggest that the evidence of mass-murder should be eaten by the perpetrators.

'Terrible things have happened all over China in recent years,' the exile told his audience, 'but in the province of Guangxi in southern China it was most certainly cannibalism. People there knew that these kind of atrocities were commonplace, and could cite instances of murder where the corpses had afterwards been eaten. Outside the province, though, very little of this was known except by the disaffected intellectuals.'

In the documents which he had secretly copied, said Zheng Yi, was the evidence of the eating of human flesh. Workers were instructed to take the law into their own hands with revisionist factory bosses when they strayed from the party line, killing them and eating the corpses. In some instances, the bodies had been displayed on meat-hooks in government-run cafeterias before being taken down and cooked. Even schoolchildren had been encouraged to murder and eat their teachers if they did not conform.

So widespread did this cannibalism become, that in 1979 some of the braver souls in Guangxi finally plucked up their courage and pinned a notice of complaint on the 'Democracy Wall' in Beijing. The notice blamed Wei Guoqing, the Party Secretary for Guangxi during the Cultural Revolution, for the atrocities and demanded compensation from the government.

According to Zheng Yi, Wei Guoqing was a friend and supporter of the Communist Party Chief, the aged Deng Xiaoping. And as soon as the complaints were registered against him, the upper echelons of power closed ranks. But not so much to protect their man in Guangxi as to prevent the stories spreading and becoming a stain on the reputation of the great Mao himself.

Wei Guoqing's days were then certainly numbered. 'In 1983, he tried to overthrow Party General Secretary Hu Yaobang,' explained Zheng Yi, 'a man who was very close to Deng Xiaoping. Wei was therefore removed from office, and all the top officials in the province who had participated in the cover-up of the events were removed. Hu Yaobang also saw to it that the stories of cannibalism were investigated, too.'

It was during these enquiries that the documents which the dissident writer smuggled to the West had been brought to light and copied. Based on them he was able to tell his press conference in New York:

'I believe that many hundreds, possibly thousands, were eaten in Guangxi. My own investigations into just one county of the province revealed that 137 people had been devoured. I think thousands must have participated in the cannibalism, too, yet no one has ever been charged or tried.

'After a while it seemed that the official action just dried up. I estimate that only about one hundred of those who participated in the cannibalism were expelled from the Party or had their pay or rank reduced. It was the most barbarous cruelty on a vast scale and ruined the lives of thousands of ordinary Chinese.'

To those in the West who read the report, it

seemed as if China had merely employed yet another brutal and even more nasty form of repression to keep the people in line – albeit a variation of an old tradition associated with parts of the world like Africa and the Pacific Islands. Yet by investigating Chinese history it does not take long to discover that cannibalism has flourished there for many thousands of years – especially at times of famine when the harvests failed. There are frequent entries of this in the ancient *Han Shu* records (published in an English translation as *Food and Money in Ancient China*) with the earliest of these accounts from the year 206 BC.

'When the House of Han arose it inherited the evils left by the Chin,' states the *Han Shu*. 'Former feudal lords all at the same time started rebellions and the people lost their means of livelihood. Hence there was a widespread dearth of supplies in both grains and vegetables. People ate human flesh, and more than half of the population died. The Founder of the Han thereupon ordered that the people be allowed to sell their children and to migrate to Shu and Han-chung for food.'

In 178 BC the story was very much the same when the level of provisions such as rice and wheat held in store was reported to be dangerously low should a famine occur.

'If war and drought come on top of each other, then the empire may come to a perilous end!' the *Han Shu* quoted a contemporary source. 'Those who are bold and have physical strength will gather followers and violently attack others. Tired and weak old men of different families will be forced to exchange the dead bodies of starved children and gnaw their bones.'

Things were no better in 87 BC according to the *Han Shu*. 'After the death of Tung Chung-shu the expenditure for various enterprises became increasingly excessive. The resources of all under Heaven were utterly wasted and again human beings ate human flesh.'

At least the emperor now took the step of appointing a minister, *Fu-min Hou* – meaning 'Marquis for Enriching the People' – charged with strengthening agricultural production. But even he could not legislate for natural disasters, and cannibalism reared its head once again in 44 BC.

'When the Emperor Yuan came to the throne there was a great flood in the empire which was especially calamitous in eleven provinces,' reads the *Han Shu*. 'In the second year crops in the territory of Chi failed and the greater part of the inhabitants starved to death. In the province of Lang-yeh residents ate human flesh.'

The same thing happened in the fief of Liang and the province of Ping-yuan in 15 BC, and was repeated again in AD 21 in Ching and Hsu. The evidence also suggests that after all these incidents of enforced cannibalism there were some people who ate human flesh for enjoyment.

In AD 25 in the province of Honan, for example, reports state that there was a whole gang of cannibals who would settle in one place and prey on the local inhabitants. It was their boast that they ate a little piece of human heart or liver at every meal. When the gang had devoured everyone in the neighbourhood they moved on somewhere new. According to contemporary reports, when news of the presence of these bloodthirsty marauders preceded them into any vicinity, whole families would abandon their homes and flee in understandable panic.

Chinese warlords also made a practice of cannibalising the bodies of their enemies during the feudal chaos which preceded the unification of China under the Han dynasty in 202 BC, according to Rene Grousett in his mammoth study, *The Rise and Splendour of the Chinese Empire* (1952).

'The struggles between the Warring States were implacable,' he writes. 'Instead of nobly holding their prisoners to ransom, from now on conquerors put them to death in mass executions. The soldiers of the kingdom of Ch'in, the most bellicose of the Warring States, received their pay only on the presentation of the severed heads of their enemies. In towns taken by assault, or even in those that capitulated, the whole population, women, old men and children were often put to the sword. Reverting once more to the cannibal practices of primitive humanity, the chiefs, in order to "increase their prestige", did not hesitate to throw their conquered enemies into boiling cauldrons and drink this horrible soup, and even force the kinsmen of their victims to drink it.'

Grousett cites an unusual instance of this among two of the main contenders for overall control of China. General Hsiang Yu had captured the father of his rival, Liu Pang, and sent word that he would boil the old man alive if his rival did not surrender. To this Liu Pang apparently replied genially, 'Hsiang Yu, you and I were formerly brothers-in-arms, so my father is thus your father, too. If you absolutely insist on boiling our father, do not forget to save me a cup of the soup.'

According to the legend, Hsiang Yu was so amused by this response that he promptly released his prisoner and had him sent back to Liu Pang with a mounted escort.

But prisoners did not often get treated with such humanity, as another French anthropologist, Pierre-Antoine Bernham, recently pointed out in an essay on ideological cannibalism in *The Times*:

'The ancient Chinese chronicles record a number of accounts of revenge, hatred and gourmandising cannibalism.' Bernham stated. 'A famous instance being that of the Emperor Wang Mang who after being defeated was killed and partly eaten by his opponents in AD 28.'

However, such stories pale into insignificance when the activities of a certain Shih Hu, who ruled the Huns of northern China between AD 334 and AD 349, are studied. Rene Grousett once again provides the facts.

'Shih Hu was a monster of debauchery,' Grousett writes, 'whose own son tried to assassinate him – and was duly executed by his father. This Tartar Bluebeard used to have the most attractive of his concubines roasted and served at table: "From time to time he used to have one of the girls of his harem beheaded, cooked and served to his guests, while the uncooked head was passed round on a plate to prove that he had not sacrificed the least beautiful," says a contemporary account. Yet with the contrast of character not uncommon among barbarians perverted by their first contact with civilisation, but capable of being reformed by the preaching of a saint, Shih Hu later became one of the most zealous protectors of Buddhism.'

Nothing, however, could abate the habit of eating human flesh in China even after the days of conflict and famine had given way to one of the world's greatest civilisations with its customs and rituals, many of which have influenced humanity throughout the rest of the world in succeeding generations. Indeed, the records show that by the tenth century human flesh was a common commodity sold openly in markets throughout the country, while restaurants serving 'Two-Legged Mutton' were to be found especially in northern China. There were a whole range of distinctively named dishes prepared from the fresh remains of men, women and even children.

Towards the end of the T'ang dynasty, in the late ninth and early tenth century, a number of Arab travellers in China substantiated these facts. 'Chinese law permits the eating of human flesh and this flesh is sold publicly,' according to M.Reinaud in his *Relation des Voyages faits par les Arabes et les Persans dan l'Indie et à la Chine dans le IXe siecle de l'Ere chrétienne*, which was published in 1845. This same volume also states that 'the Chinese eat the flesh of all men who are executed by the sword'.

In his study of *Daily Life in China, 1250-1276*, Jacques Gernet says that customers travelled from far and wide to the busy, sophisticated southern capital of Hangchow to dine at the human-flesh restaurants. He also explains how this apparently revolting concept fitted into the Chinese way of life:

'There is another reason for the excellence and variety of Chinese cooking,' Gernet says, 'it is based on ancient peasant traditions which arose in rural surroundings where undernourishment, drought and famines were frequent, and so it makes judicious use of every possible kind of edible vegetable and insect as well as of offal. There is no doubt that in this sphere China has shown a greater inventiveness than any other civilisation. It is also to be noted that there were no religious taboos about food. Only fervent Buddhists and ascetic Taoists abstained, the former from eating vegetables with a strong smell (onions and garlic), meat and eggs; the latter from cereals. Milk and cheese were absent from the diet, but this was because there had never been any dairy farming in China.

'For the same reason, Hangchow people did not

eat beef: the ox was the farmer's faithful companion. Moreover, it was an animal that was scarce and dear to buy, even in the north, and it did not acclimatise so well in the warm, humid climate of the lower Yangtze as the water buffalo. As for human flesh, it was perhaps not the object of such violent repulsion as is the case in the West. One author relates – deploring the fact it is true – that people from north China, where habits of cannibalism had spread after the wars and famines, had opened restaurants in Hangchow where human flesh was served. Dishes made from the flesh of women, old men, young girls and children each had a special name and were served in the same way as mutton – human flesh in general being euphemistically called "two-legged mutton".'

References to dining on human flesh can be found in a number of Chinese works of literature. In the *Chou Hou Chouen* (The Story of the River Banks), for instance, the following paragraph appears:

'The hostess then cheerfully served up the supper and the two bowmen, spurred on by hunger, began to eat. But Wou-song, who had opened a pie and was examining it with care, interrogated her.

"Are these man pies or dog pies?" he demanded.

"Man pies!" the hostess replied with a cry of laughter. "Where would we get human meat to make pies these days? The country is quiet. There are no wars on just now!"'

In another work, the *San Kui Chi* (The History of Three Kingdoms), a huntsman who has had an unsuccessful day returns home with no game to find that a great man named Hsuan-te has arrived and is staying for dinner.

'So the huntsman had no alternative but to kill his wife to allay the hunger of Hsuan-te,' the book says, 'and when Hsuan-te asked, "What is this meat?", the man replied simply, "Wolf". And they supped.'

The practice of cannibalism in China continued unabated with the opening of the nation to visitors and missionaries from the West in the eighteenth and nineteenth century. According to E H Parker writing in the *China Review* in February 1901, it was not unusual for Chinese children to show filial piety to their ailing parents by offering them their own flesh and blood in order to help them recover.

'In the 1870s, two cases were reported in the Chinese newspaper,' said Mr Parker, 'one in which a son cut a piece of flesh from his arm to make soup for his ailing mother (who recovered), and the other concerning a girl who placed a piece of her own flesh in her dying father's medicine. He, too, recovered. And when he went to his ancestors ten years later, the girl pined away and died.'

A number of Christian missionaries from Europe and America who penetrated into the furthermost reaches of the nation were also eaten for their pains. This cannibalism was viewed as a kind of gruesome backhanded compliment, because the flesh-eaters considered the men to be brave and resourceful and hoped to ingest their strength by eating them. In one southerly province near the border of Indo-China, the heart and brains of a Catholic missionary and a well-known robber chieftain who were both captured on the same day were eaten side by side at the same meal.

The *North China Mail* in 1890 also reported that, 'No Chinese soldier in Tonking during the late war lost an opportunity to eat the flesh of a fallen French foe, believing that human flesh, especially that of foreign warriors, is the best stimulant for a man's courage.' The same source retold the story of the people of a place called Kwang-si who in 1901 boiled and ate a Chinese officer 'who had been sent to pacify them'!

And so the story goes on to this day, according to reports by people like Zheng Yi which opened this last chapter in my study of the world's flesh-eaters. Though the visitor to China may find it difficult to see actual evidence of the tradition continuing, the same is certainly not true in the trade of animal flesh.

In Canton, for instance, just a little off the tourist trail, there are numerous markets and restaurants to be found where dogs, cats, tortoises, guinea pigs, raccoons, rabbits, frogs, foxes, wild boar and even snakes and rats are all readily available for sale and consumption.

At the restaurants, the delicacies on offer to diners include Braised Guinea Pig (whole) with Mashed Shrimp, Steamed Cat, Shredded Wildcat Thick Soup, Dog Meat ('ready to be cooked in an earthen pot over a charcoal stove at your table') as well as Double Boiled Sliced Deer's Blood-Rong, Sautéed Sliced Peacock and Shredded Mud-Puppy. It is not without good reason, it seems to me, that there is a wry remark heard about the Cantonese and the southern Chinese in general that they will eat everything with legs, 'except the table and chairs'.

The Man Who Made Zombies

Flat 213 in the block known as Oxford Apartments on North 25th Street in Milwaukee was ostensibly like thousands of others in the poorer areas of the sprawling city located on the western shore of Lake Michigan. As the largest city in the state of Wisconsin it was famous as a blue collar town because of its breweries and large number of great manufacturing companies including the motorcycle makers, Harley Davidson, many of which provided employment for the men and women who lived in apartments like 213.

The resident of the flat was known to be a single white man and was not seen a great deal by his mainly black and immigrant neighbours, apparently being rather shy and preferring to keep to himself. He was known to work at the huge Ambrosia Chocolate Factory at 12500 West Carmen Avenue, which had been making sweet products to sell all over the nation since 1894. The plant gave off an unmistakable smell of bubbling chocolate that was familiar to everyone in the surrounding districts.

It would, though, be a very different scent that would turn Flat 213 into an international focus of disgust and horror when the story of its occupant became common knowledge. Certainly, there were a few people in North 25th Street who had suspicions about the young man who was thought to be gay and have an unhealthy interest in the darker areas of the occult. One rumour suggested he had built a shrine in his flat to seek the powers of evil and how these might be harnessed to influence his life. Another whispered he had some weird theories about zombies and actually wanted to create his own 'dead men alive'.

In fact, what the well-spoken, reserved and intelligent young man, Jeffrey Dahmer, was doing behind his locked black door was far worse than any of this gossip and in 1992 he was revealed to be among the worst serial killers in America and a practitioner of cannibalism, too . . .

Milwaukee, where these events occurred, was originally inhabited by a number of Indian tribes including the Potawatomi, Winnebago and Macouten, and got its name from an Indian word, *Millioke*, meaning 'Good Land.' Founded originally in 1818 by a Frenchman, Solomon Juneau, German immigrants helped to bolster the population in the 1840s and today the metropolitan area is home to almost 1,700,000 people of various nationalities and races and is the nineteenth largest city in the United States.

'Good Land' it indeed seems to be to many of these inhabitants with all its industries to provide employment. Despite the working class image, it also has a major zoo, several museums and theatres and each year hosts the largest music festival in the world, Summerfest, attracting a million visitors, which has earned Milwaukee the title 'City of Festivals.' There was, though, nothing good or to celebrate when the story of 'The Man Who Wanted To Make Zombies' came to court with the charges that he had killed at least fifteen men between 1978 and 1991, the majority of them young, homosexual black men. It proved to be a blood-curdling saga of murders that had its origins in the pale, blond-haired, moustached young man's childhood.

Jeffrey Lionel Dahmer was born on 21 May 1960 in Milwaukee, the only son of Lionel and Joyce Dahmer, both fundamentalist Christians. In 1960, the family moved to the picturesque, upmarket town of Bath near Akron in Ohio, where Jeffrey showed no obvious signs of being anything other than a rather frail, if extremely shy child. At school, however, the change in his character began in 1968 when he was sexually molested by another boy. Unreported at the time, it has been suggested that this childhood incident so traumatised Dahmer that it eventually lead to his life of serial killings.

It would also not be known until his trial that by the age of ten he was 'experimenting with dead animals, decapitating rodents, bleaching chicken bones with acid and had nailed a dog's carcass to a tree and mounted its head on a stake,' according to a statement read out in court. Several neighbours were believed to have seen the evidence of the boy's nauseating attempts at taxidermy on animals killed on the local roads, but did not report the facts to either animal welfare or social services. Jeffrey was also said to have shown an interest in necrophilia as early as the age of fourteen – having fantasies about killing men and having sex with their corpses.

These dark thoughts that were running amok in his mind were not helped by the unhappiness in his home, where Lionel and Joyce Dahmer frequently had terrible arguments, leading to their divorce when Jeffrey was still a teenager. His already low-esteem plummeted even further and he began the secretive drinking which would ultimately turn him into an alcoholic. However, it was just after he had graduated in June 1978 that Jeffrey Dahmer turned from killing and experimenting on animals to human beings.

The Dahmer parents had just left the family home in Bath, neither one prepared to take their teenage son with them until their acrimonious divorce had been settled. Left to his own weird inclinations, Jeffrey one day bumped into a dark-haired, handsome young boy, Steven Hicks, who was hitch-hiking across Ohio. He invited Steve back to his house for 'some fun and a few beers.' It is claimed the couple had sex, although it seems more likely that Dahmer was still a repressed homosexual at this time. What happened, though, that day undoubtedly contributed to his deadly hatred of gays.

When Jeffrey tried to encourage Hicks to stay on in the house with him and the young hitch-hiker refused, he felt the pain of rejection again. He had plenty of money, he said, and they could have a good time. But Hicks was adamant. As he turned to leave the house, Dahmer who could not bear the idea of letting his new 'friend' go, struck him from behind with a barbell. He finished the killing by strangling his victim and then sat down to consider what he should do with the body.

After all the years of experimenting with animals, Jeffrey Dahmer was not short of ideas. Undisturbed in the house, he cut the boy's corpse up into small pieces and then packaged them all in black rubbish bags. These he buried in the woods behind his home.

The evidence suggests that this first killing shocked young Jeffrey into a semblance of normality for a while. Following a summer living alone with his guilty secret, he enrolled at Ohio State University in the autumn. However, he performed poorly, made few friends, and shortly afterwards quit the course. In December 1978, Lionel Dahmer, who was now divorced, came back into his son's life and encouraged him to join the army.

The following year, Jeffrey was stationed in Germany where he appeared to 'gain some vitality,' according to one report. But he was not popular with the other men and the drinking which had grown excessive now turned into full-blown alcoholism. It was not long before the Army brass could see only one course of action where this particular soldier who was perennially drunk was concerned.

Two years after he had signed up, Dahmer was discharged and sent back to America. Long after he had left Germany, when he was revealed as a serial killer, a number of unsolved murders in the area where he had been stationed became the subject of speculation that he might have been the killer. There is, however, no concrete evidence to connect him with the crimes and he certainly made no mention of them in his full confession to the police.

On his return to the States, Jeffrey Dahmer did not go back to Ohio, but to the city where he had been born. Here, at the urging of his father, he went to live with his grandmother at her house in the Milwaukee suburb of West Allis where he was made welcome to stay. The sympathetic old lady gave him his own room and allowed him the freedom to come and go as he chose.

The fantasies which had plagued Dahmer's childhood and lead to his killing the hitch-hiker soon returned, initially in a less violent form.

According to one version of events, this new phase of his life was triggered after he had returned to the woods where he buried the body of Steven Hicks. For some reason known only to his morbid self, he dug up the decomposing corpse, pounded the remains with a sledgehammer into tiny pieces and scattered the residue in the undergrowth.

Dahmer then got himself a job at the Ambrosia Chocolate Factory. Here he was set to work on a mixer in the enormous plant that manufactured the basic chocolate for use in all types of products for worldwide distribution. For a while, Jeffrey was intoxicated by the rich, sweet smell that rose from the huge vats and wafted through the building into the streets beyond. He found some of the bars produced from this chocolate irresistible – especially the famous Stone Mountain Gourmet Fudge – and thoughts of how he might use these sweetmeats to his advantage began to drift through his mind like the scent from the vats. It was around this time, too, that Jeffrey Dahmer got his first taste of the Milwaukee gay bars . . .

In August 1982, on one of his days off from the factory, Dahmer went to the Summerfest on the shore of Lake Michigan. There he apparently wandered amongst the thousands of visitors – increasingly aroused by their sweaty proximity and his own inner fantasies. Police records indicate that he was arrested during the fair for 'indecent exposure', having dropped his trousers in front of a group of people. He may well also have been drunk at the time, but there is no record of a charge being brought against him.

Four years passed before Dahmer was in trouble with the law again. In September 1986, two boys told a policeman in West Allis that a man had exposed himself to them and masturbated. Their description of the person with his pale features and drooping moustache quickly enabled the officer to match the facts to the earlier run-in at the Summerfest. This time, though, Dahmer was taken to court and convicted of 'disorderly conduct,' given a one year suspended sentence and ordered to seek counselling.

The day of infamy that would result in Jeffrey Dahmer's second murder and the beginning of his spree of deaths occurred on Tuesday 15 September 1987. It followed a night of drinking in one of the popular gay bars where he met another dark-haired handsome young man named Steven Toumi. The couple eventually staggered from the bar and booked into a nearby hotel. The next morning when he awoke, Jeffrey said he found Toumi dead in the bed with blood all around his mouth.

This death would remain unknown until Dahmer's arrest. Even then he claimed he did not know how Toumi had died. He admitted, though, that he had bought a large suitcase and put the body inside. This he took to his grandmother's flat in West Allis and hid in the basement. Later, he said, he had sex with the corpse and masturbated over it. After dark, the killer dismembered Toumi's body and packed the pieces in the garbage cans, which were carried away without a hint of suspicion.

Whatever the truth of Dahmer's claims, this second killing seems to have excited his homicidal tendencies – and plunge him into cannibalism with his later victims. The next of these was a fourteen-year-old Native American boy named Jamie Doxtator who was known to hang around outside the city's gay bars looking for 'relationships.' In January 1988 it was his misfortune to catch the eye of Jeffrey Dahmer and fall victim to what thereafter became the chocolate factory worker's modus operandi.

Dahmer offered $50 to the dark-skinned, engaging young man if he would pose for photo-graphs. If Jamie – or any of those who followed in his stead – were at all reluctant, he would instead invite them to his flat to watch a video and just have a beer or two. Once the victims had been lured back to his room, he drugged their beer and strangled them. After having sex with the corpse and masturbating over it, the bodies were dismem-bered with a hacksaw and the remains disposed of.

With the attractively chocolate-coloured Jamie Doxtator he was first tempted to taste human flesh. Dahmer also licked some of the boy's blood – though the taste did not particularly appeal to him – and discovered the whole experience gave him a new thrill. He also decided to keep his victim's skull and some other unspecified parts of the boy's body – probably his sexual organs.

In March 1988, Dahmer trapped another handsome young victim, Richard Guerero of Mexican origin, who he claimed to have met at a gay bar in Milwaukee. When the young man's family were later told of the events of their son's death, however, they denied that he had ever been gay. Whatever the truth, Guerero was drugged, stabbed and several parts of his anatomy put into Dahmer's freezer. Jeffrey took particular care with the Mexican's biceps and other muscles, freezing them so that he could eat them later.

Despite the care he took in disposing of his victims, Jeffrey Dahmer could not conceal all his nocturnal activities from his grandmother. She put up with his drinking and the odd friends he brought to the house late at night. However, she knew nothing of what was going on in the basement, beyond Jeffrey's off-hand remarks that he was conducting 'experiments.' Finally, she found the stench creeping up into her rooms too much to bear and told Jeffrey to leave. On 25 September he moved into an apartment on North 24th Street and within a day had been unable to resist the pull of his old fantasies.

With his usual offer of money to model for some photographs, he lured a young Laotian boy, thirteen-year-old Sounth Sinthasomphone, to visit his flat. It was a million-to-one chance that he should have picked this particular boy – and one of the strangest coincidences ever recorded in the annals of serial killing and cannibalism – that Sounth was the older brother of Konerak Sinthasomphone who he was destined to kill in May 1991 in his final flurry of mayhem before justice finally caught up with him.

Once in the apartment, Dahmer drugged the boy and fondled his genitals – rather more gently than usual, examination later would reveal – and with no attempt to have intercourse with him. When the boy recovered consciousness he was allowed to go home, none the wiser as to what had happened to him. The Sinthasomphone parents were, though, understandably suspicious of his dazed condition and took him to hospital. There a doctor confirmed the teenager had been drugged and the police were summoned to take a statement of everything the boy could remember.

Within a few hours, Jeffrey Dahmer had been picked up by two detectives while he was busy working on his shift at the Ambrosia Chocolate factory. He was arrested and charged with second-degree sexual assault and the exploitation of a child. On 30 January 1989 he appeared in court and pleaded guilty to the charge, offering the mitigating circumstances that he thought the boy was older than thirteen. He was freed to await formal sentencing scheduled for May. In the interim, he was to return to live with his long-suffering grandmother once again.

While Jeffrey Dahmer awaited the verdict of the

court in the spring of 1989, the old urges returned. Although his grandmother was trying to keep a closer watch on his movements, this was no easy task for an old lady, and less than two months later, on 25 March, he spread his web of deceit around a twenty-four-year-old black man he met in a gay bar.

The new victim's name was Anthony Sears, a smartly dressed, good-looking man who was trying to make a career as a male model. Dahmer offered him money to pose for photographs and the two men walked the short distance to old Mrs Dahmer's house. There the hapless Sears was drugged and strangled and once again Dahmer committed necrophilia and cannibalism on the body before dismembering it.

On this occasion, though, the killer added a new and grisly element to his repertoire of ways for getting rid of the corpse. After disposing of the skeleton, organs and flesh, he boiled the skull until all the skin had been removed and then painted it grey so that if it was ever discovered, it would appear to be one of the plastic models used by medical students during training. When this skull and several others treated in the same way were later found in Apartment 2123, Dahmer admitted that they were real and he liked to use them for sexual gratification when he masturbated.

The officials in the Milwaukee court were, of course, completely unaware of this latest killing when Jeffrey Dahmer returned for sentencing on

23 May on the molestation charge. Three psychologists who had examined him in the interim gave testimony to Judge William Gardner that the prisoner was manipulative, resistant and evasive. His only perception of having done anything wrong was that he had chosen a victim who was too young. Dahmer, they all agreed, was 'unwilling or incapable of dealing with his deepseated psychological problems.' The prosecution demanded that he be sent to prison for at least five years; the defence argued that he was mentally ill and should be hospitalised for treatment.

Jeffrey himself was given the opportunity to address the court and put the blame for his actions on his alcoholism. He said earnestly that he had never done anything like this before and if he was allowed to go free he had one thing that he believed would help him to come out of his 'nightmare' – his job at the chocolate factory.

'The one thing I have in my mind that is stable and gives me some source of pride is my job,' he told Judge Gardner. 'I've come very close to losing it because of my actions, for which I take full responsibility. All I can do is beg you, please spare my job. Please give me a chance to show that I can tread the straight and narrow and not get involved in any situation like this ever again. This enticing a child was the climax of my idiocy.'

Few serial killers have ever had the audacity – or opportunity – to make such a claim and emerge virtually free men. Despite receiving a letter from

Dahmer's stricken father urging that his son be confined and not released until he had received treatment, the Judge stayed the sentence. The accused was to be put on probation for five years and would spend one year in the House of Correction under a 'work release.' This would enable him to go to the chocolate factory during the day and return to the institution at night. The sentence would prove to be anything *but* a climax to his actions.

Ten months later, in March 1990, Dahmer was released on the understanding that he returned initially to his grandmother's house. The agreement was also conditional on him looking for his own place to live. On 14 May he moved into Flat 213 and a saga of killings began such as the city of Milwaukee had never experienced before.

The first of what would ultimately be a dozen murders in the next fifteen months, began with black homosexual Edward Smith four weeks later in June. The next month it was another Smith – no relation – named Raymond Smith who was lured to Dahmer's apartment and subjected to the familiar butchery and cannibalism. Three more victims were slaughtered in the next three months, Ricky Lee Beeks, Ernest Miller and then David Thomas in late September.

It was during this very hot summer that Jeffrey Dahmer conceived his extraordinary idea of creating zombies who would become live-in sex toys, obedient to his every desire. He had, of course, been conducting 'experiments' on animals since his childhood and now decided to try the same on humans. Although Dahmer was already deeply into the occult and voodoo, he wanted to use more direct methods and by his own admission began 'lobotomising' several of his victims.

After he had drugged the man, he drilled a hole into the skull and dribbled a solution of muriatic acid into the brain. This, he believed, would destroy the subject's conscious will and make them obey his every command. Although the mad amateur neurosurgeon claimed that one victim had 'actually functioned minimally like a zombie for several days,' there is little doubt that all of these unfortunate victims died instantly.

If any of Dahmer's victims had any suspicions that he might be a bit odd before they entered his apartment, these were quickly confirmed when they saw the shrine he had built in one corner of the living room. On this stood several skulls, the statue of a griffin, black candles and a number of sticks of incense. Other 'trophies' would later find a place on this shrine – including human bones and organs – all of which he hoped would give him, 'special powers and energies to help me socially and financially.' Dahmer also spent a lot of time deliberating on the nature of good and evil.

'Having the bodies of the men around me made me feel thoroughly evil,' he later told a police detective while he was being interviewed 'I have to question whether there is an evil force in the world and whether or not I have been influenced by it. Although I am not sure if there is a God or if there is a devil, I know that lately I've been doing a lot of thinking about both.'

He was also thinking about more victims to feed his sexual and cannibal lusts. In February 1991, Dahmer began what would prove to be his final, frenzied spree by killing Curtis Straughter. This hapless victim was followed by Errol Lindsey in April and Tony Hughes in May. Each was done to death in the same manner, although Jeffrey would sometimes use his bare hands or a leather strap to strangle the man.

The police recovered evidence later that dated from this period and revealed Dahmer had taken Polaroid pictures of each stage of his victim's death – including the sexually explicit acts he performed on their bodies. After dismembering the corpses, he used various chemicals and acids to reduce the remaining bones and organs to a 'slurry' that he could flush down the toilet or pour away in the sink.

The man who tried to make automatons also confessed that eating human flesh when it was freshly cut from a body gave him an erection. He even used various seasonings and meat tenderisers on the flesh to make it more tasty. And in order not to waste any choice items, he put strips of flesh from several of his victims into his freezer to eat later. A few items, notably the genitals, he preserved in formaldehyde in order to have something left just to savour his triumph. Dahmer claimed that by doing this the people he had eaten would come alive in him and redouble his energy.

As this carnage continued, however, Dahmer came within a heart beat of being caught. In the early hours of 27 May, two teenage black girls, Nicole Childress and Sandra Smith, summoned the police to North 25th Street, after they found a young Laotian boy naked, bleeding and muttering uncontrollably in the road.

While the two officers were cross-questioning the girls and trying to make sense of the youngster's ramblings, Jeffrey Dahmer stepped out of the nearby Oxford Apartments Block. Speaking quite calmly, he informed the policemen that the boy was his 'adult homosexual lover' and he had run off after they had 'a lover's tiff.' Dahmer added that the boy was nineteen, but had not yet learned to speak English, which was why he could not answer any of their questions.

The police records indicate that the two oficers accepted Dahmer's story and despite the boy's evident fear of his 'lover' – not to mention the unease of the two girls about the tall white man – they allowed the pair to return to Apartment 613. The boy's name was Konerak Sinthasomphone, he was actually just thirteen years old, and by the cruellest twist of fate was the younger brother of Sounth Sinthasomphone who had escaped from the serial killer's clutches in September 1988. Konerak, though, would never be seen alive again.

Evidently untroubled about yet another brush with the law, Dahmer killed his next victim on 30 June (Matt Turner) . . . then struck again on 5 July (Jeremiah Weinberger) . . . once more on 12 July (Oliver Lacy)…and yet again on 19 July when Joseph Bradehoft suffered the same agonies and fate as his predecessors.

Then, just two days later, on 22 July, in scenes that were curiously reminiscent of the incident with the Laotian boy, a black man was seen stumbling along North 25th Street by two officers in a patrol car. At first glance he might have seemed like just another drunk on his way home after a night out – but the blood on his face and the handcuffs hanging from one wrist convinced the officers otherwise.

According to a subsequent report in the *Milwaukee Journal*, the man, identified as Tracy Edwards (thirty-two), told the officers he had been invited to the flat of a 'weird dude' who had put on a video and given him a couple of drinks that made him feel sleepy. He had then been handcuffed, threatened with a knife and told that unless he co-operated he would 'have his heart cut out and eaten.' Although Edwards felt as if he was going to fall unconscious at any moment, he managed to punch the 'dude' and escape from the flat, still wearing the handcuffs.

Edwards lead the officers back to the flat where Dahmer tried to keep them at the door. He had just lost his job at Ambrose's, he said, had got drunk and then lost his temper when Edwards would not co-operate in some sex games. He would go and get the keys and release the handcuffs.

Now thoroughly suspicious, one of the officers followed Dahmer into the flat. It was the stench that first alerted him. Then, as he followed the tenant into his bedroom, it was the dozens of Polaroid photographs of dismembered bodies stuck all over the walls. In the kitchen he saw the same refrigerator that was featured in the pictures and gingerly opened the door. Inside a human head stood on the top shelf.

In that moment the career of the serial killer who wanted to create the living dead came to an end. Although the two officers were absolutely revolted by the horrors all around them, they acted as one and soon had Dahmer pinned to the floor, screaming and protesting, while they handcuffed him.

A search of the flat by forensic officers brought to light one gruesome relic after another. In the freezer, bags of human flesh were found along with three more human skulls. In a stockpot in the kitchen floated several human hands and a penis; and in two other jars several male genitalia lay preserved in a yellow liquid. In the sink and toilet were found traces of human flesh and bone splinters that had all contributed to the terrible stench in the apartment of death. And in all, the police found traces of no less than eleven distinct bodies.

Painstaking and stomach-turning work by

Detective Patrick Kennedy of the Milwaukee force at both the crime scene and in the basement of Dahmer's grandmother's house in West Allis produced further evidence that at least fifteen men had been killed by the former chocolate factory worker. Kennedy's skill as an interviewer and his ability to win the confidence of Jeffrey Dahmer also drew pages of confession from the prisoner about his thirteen year killing spree. Even the big veteran Irish-American cop with his bristling handlebar moustache came near to being physically sick as he sat listening to his prisoner's catalogue of murder and cannibalism.

The subsequent court case, which began on 30 January 1992, horrified America and almost made the name Dahmer synonymous with serial killer. Secured behind an eighteen-foot-high steel barrier, he entered a plea of guilty but insane to the charge of fifteen counts of murder. However, after two weeks of hearing nauseating evidence, the jury found the prisoner sane and responsible for his actions. He was sentenced to fifteen consecutive life terms – a minimum of nine hundred and thirty-six years imprisonment – as Wisconsin has no capital punishment.

History – and in particular the history of cannibalism – had not quite finished with Jeffrey Dahmer, though. In the Columbia Correctional Institute at Portage, Wisconsin he was offered protective custody because of the numerous threats made against him by other prisoners, but he steadfastly refused. Even the attempt by one convict to slash his throat in the prison chapel could not change his mind.

However, on 28 November 1994, while Dahmer was cleaning out a bathroom adjacent to the prison gym, a twenty-five-year-old prisoner, Christopher Scarver, a black delusional schizophrenic who believed himself to be the 'son of God,' jumped on the serial killer and beat him to death with an iron bar not unlike the barbell with which he had slain his very first victim, Steven Hicks. Before Dahmer's funeral, a request was made to his father for permission to use his son's brain for scientific purposes, but this was declined on religious grounds – although the broken man did help in the case study and wrote his revealing autobiography, *A Father's Story* (1993).

Two years later, in 1996, the city elders of Milwaukee decided to buy Jeffrey Dahmer's now notorious collection of Polaroid photographs, tools and refrigerator, for fear that they might be sold and turned into a museum. According to the *Milwaukee Journal*, the items were purchased for $400,000 and immediately incinerated. It was hoped, a leader in the paper added, that this action would 'lay to rest the grisly ghosts that haunt our city.'

The Ripper of Rostov

Rostov-on-Don near the Black Sea is a famous
Russian seaport steeped in history. Named
originally 'Rostov which lies on the River Don' to
distinguish it from the ancient north Russian city
in the Yaroslavl Region, it stands on a site that is
sacred to the people because it was here that the
famous Don Cossacks – serfs who had fled to the
Don to escape the oppression of their masters –
courageously defended the southern frontier of
Russia. For centuries its fortress of Dmitry
Rostovsky, with its redoubts, bastions and
cannons, was the largest on the south of the
country and provided a barrier against invaders
from the Sea of Azov and a haven for fleeing
Armenians, Jews, Poles and many others.

Despite its history of bloodshed and the fact that
the Don is frozen for more than a hundred days a
year, the city has grown to become one of the

biggest industrial centres in the county, exporting vast quantities of grain, vegetable oils and raw wool and manufacturing everything from agricultural machinery and helicopters to tobacco products, shoes and even champagne. It also has the dubious distinction of being the place where the 'Rostov Ripper' carried out his reign of terror, murdering at least fifty-three young girls and boys between 1978 and 1990 and becoming the worst serial killer in Russian history.

The man's name was Andrei Chikatilo and he is known in the country as 'The Forest Strip Killer' – and occasionally as 'The Shelter Belt Killer,' because of the number of corpses he discarded in woods alongside railway lines – and in the west as 'The Russian Hannibal Lecter.' However, in some early Soviet accounts of his life, in which he is referred to as 'Citizen X,' Chikatilo was *not* a serial killer – such people did not exist in the Communist State. They were, 'the product of the decadent and corrupt west,' to quote the party line. It was not, in fact, until he was finally caught and executed in 1994 that the whole story began to spread beyond the confines of Rostov and the Ukraine. Indeed, news of his execution was the first many people knew about the man who has been compared to the unknown killer who stalked the streets of London almost a century earlier . . . yet he was infinitely worse.

Although today Rostov-on-Don is a prosperous city with its own university, research centres, botanical gardens, libraries and Sports Palace, it also has daunting blocks of bureaucratic buildings and law offices from its Communist past. On some of these can still be seen the scars from the Nazi occupation during the Second World War when Russia was fighting for her very existence against Hitler's troops hell-bent on taking Stalingrad, just 250 miles to the north. In their fury at being beaten by the bravery of the Russian troops and the intense cold of the winter, the Germans set fire to many buildings including the magnificent Gorky Drama Theatre, a palace of glass and marble, which has thankfully since been restored.

At the heart of Rostov lies the grim Central Prison with its euphemistically entitled but notorious execution chamber 'Pistol Target Room No. 3.' It was here that Chikatilo met his end on 14 February 1994. Although legend has it that condemned prisoners are made to kneel on the dank, concrete floor to be shot, they are in fact strapped into a large wooden chair fixed into this floor – a device not unlike the American electric chair. Behind the chair stands a high wall of sand bags and a channel made of zinc to catch the prisoner's blood.

On that February morning, Andrei Chikatilo was reported to have been brought into the room, 'shouting curses and obscenities at his executioners.' As was traditional, the executioner was a volunteer from the prison staff who did not see his target until the man was securely bound into the chair. Then, after the death sentence had been formally read to the prisoner by the Principal of the prison, the staff member – wearing carpet slippers so that his approach would not be heard – walked towards Chikatilo from the rear. 'The Rostov Ripper' was still hurling abuse at all those around him as the barrel of a Makarov 9mm service pistol was pressed behind his right ear and fired.

The 'nine gram treatment' – as this form of execution is known in Russia, after the weight of the bullet – blew blood and brain tissue onto the sand bag wall and killed Chikatilo instantly. He was certified dead by the prison doctor and there only remained the task of cremating the body of the country's worst ever killer. Such, though, was the damage to the executed man's brain that even if the authorities had agreed to the approach by a Japanese scientific group to buy it for study – similar, in fact, to the request made to city fathers of Milwaukee for Jeffrey Dahmer's brain – there was actually little left recognisable of his head as he went to his unmourned death . . .

The life of Andrei Romanovich Chikatilo was as nasty and brutish as the grief he brought to his victims and their families. Born in the Ukraine on 16 October 1936, he grew up in the town of Novocherkassk less than 25 miles from Rostov which also had a similar bloody history, largely associated with the macho culture of the Cossacks.

The area was also hit badly by the great period of upheaval caused by Stalin's policy of collectivisation that caused millions to die of starvation and cannibalism became rife among the most desperate.

The Chikatilo family suffered the famine like everyone else and during his childhood, young Andrei was repeatedly told a story by his mother than an older brother, Stepan, had been kidnapped and eaten by starving neighbours. Although no record of a Stepan Chikatilo's birth or death has ever been found, the story was told with such hysterical fervour that none of the other children dared disbelieve their mother. Andrei claimed later that when he was five his village had been overrun by German troops and his father, Roman, had been taken off to a prisoner of war camp. He also had to stand by helplessly while a group of German soldiers gang raped his mother.

As if these traumas were not enough to scar the child for life, he was also severely near-sighted, rather effeminate and regularly wet his bed until he was a teenager. At school he was bullied unmercifully every day for all these failings. Trying unsuccessfully to live up to the image of the Cossack tradition as all Rostov boys did, he turned gradually to degenerate and perverted behaviour. When periodic sexual impotence was added to his list of problems and he was unable to get an erection, he sought relief in masturbation.

The misery of Chikatilo's schooldays was only

redoubled when, at nineteen, he was called up to join the army. Here again he was taunted about his appearance and accused of being a homosexual. He claimed to have been raped by other soldiers on more than one occasion.

When Chikatilo left the army he returned to Rostov and tried his luck again with girls in the hope of proving his sexuality. He began dating, looking for meek and submissive girls, but soon found the reality very different. Finally, after great persistence with one girl, she agreed to go to bed with him. The result was a disaster: once again he was unable to get an erection and the girl left his room laughing, eager to tell all her friends. In that moment, Andrei Chikatilo experienced for the first time the hatred of the female sex that would drive him into acts of terrible violence.

Yet despite his afflictions – Chikatilo was convinced that he had been half-blinded and castrated from birth – he tried to make the best of his life, becoming a loyal member of the Communist Party and obtaining a job as a telephone engineer at Rodionovo-Nesvatayevesky, a few miles from Rostov. When he was caught masturbating by a colleague, he again felt the power of ridicule.

In 1963, at the age of twenty-seven, Andrei's sister introduced him to a twenty-four-year-old local girl, Fayina Feodosia, and after a whirlwind courtship the couple married. Although it was soon obvious to the young bride that her husband had a very inadequate and distorted sex drive, the couple did produce two children, Ludmila and Yuri. When Andrei took a correspondence course and obtained degrees in Engineering, Russian Literature and Marxism-Leninism, he was to all *outside* appearances a model worker and father. Indeed, he even tried to raise his status by applying for – and getting – a post at an all-male mining school in Rostov.

The façade of respectability that Chikatilo had been building up started to fall apart almost as soon as he began teaching. His weakness and shyness made him unable to gain the respect of either his colleagues – who considered him 'odd' – or the pupils who heckled him unmercifully from the first day he entered a classroom. He was quickly nicknamed 'Goose' because of his long neck and slouching posture.

When Chikatilo was put on night duty and had to make the rounds of the boys' dormitories to put the lights out, he fell prey to his inner demons. Ostensibly tucking in the sheets of the boys' beds, he began molesting the smaller pupils and soon had the word 'faggot' being whispered behind his back every time he passed. Then he was caught trying to perform oral sex on one sleeping boy by a group of older boys who beat him up unmercifully. Despite his age and size, Chikatilo was undoubtedly terrified of his charges and began to carry a knife in his pocket for fear of attack.

In the mid-seventies, several complaints were

made against him and he was forced to resign. Because of the Soviet system of the time, any indiscretions by staff were said to reflect badly on a school, so no charges were brought against him. In 1978, Chikatilo managed to obtain a new post at a mixed boarding school in Novo Shatinsk. Here he could hardly avoid seeing the first sexual encounters between the pubescent boys and girls and realised what he had missed in his own youth.

At first, Chikatilo seemed content to surreptitiously fondle the girls while they were swimming. This continued until one screamed and alerted the others. Shortly after, he kept a fourteen-year-old girl behind in detention and beat her with a ruler until he ejaculated. Still his feelings of frustration and bitterness continued to grow until finally he felt compelled to let his demons really have free rein.

As would later be pointed out, Chikatilo was much older than most men who became serial killers. Research of cases over the last two centuries has shown that repeat killers normally begin hunting their victims when still in their early twenties. Chikatilo, though, would be over forty-two when the first children began to go missing in and around Rostov-on-Don . . .

The lower reaches of the River Don are very beautiful, an area of tranquil lagoons ringed by thickets of wood and bushes. The place is much loved by local people. The old go there to sit and rest away from the hustle and bustle of the city; the young and in love to find seclusion and a little time for romance far away from intrusive eyes. Unfortunately, though, this would become the haunt of *Lesopolosa* – the 'Forest Strip Killer.'

The killer's first victim was nine-year-old Lenochka Zakotnova – Lena for short – who had been walking home through the suburb of Shakhty on the evening of 22 December. Approached by a tall, thin, middle-aged man who offered her a sweet, the little girl was lured to a vacant house beside the Grushevka River where she was forced to the ground and her clothes ripped off. After failing to penetrate the girl, the attacker slashed and stabbed her until he climaxed. Chikatilo had found the key to his own brand of sexual ecstasy: domination, mutilation and then satisfaction when he finally stabbed the girl to death. Little Lena's body was then unceremoniously thrown into the nearby river where it was not found until Christmas Eve.

The resulting police investigation threw up several suspects including Andrei Chikatilo who had actually been seen with Lena by another child. An artist's impression made from the girl's description of the killer matched the teacher's features and blood was also discovered on the steps of the vacant riverside house, which he was found to own. Two detectives interviewed Chikatilo and the career of the man who would ultimately kill over fifty more victims *could* have been ended at that moment. But for reasons that have never been fully explained, Fayina Chikatilo insisted her husband was at home all night on the day in question.

Suspicion then turned to another convicted child rape-slayer, twenty-five-year-old Alexandr Kravchenko, who could not satisfactorily account for his movements on the night of 22 December. Although he denied responsibility despite brutal police interrogation, his wife took a different view to that of Fayina Chikatilo and testified against him. Initially sentenced to fifteen years in prison, protests by the outraged Zakotnova family had this thrown out by a higher court and Kravchenko made the one-way journey to 'Pistol Target Room No. 3' that should, in truth, have been the destination of Andrei Chikatilo.

The case was given little publicity beyond the confines of Rostov because of the tight controls then exerted on the Soviet media. Indeed, it would be several years before anyone was prepared to admit there might have been a miscarriage of justice and that after the events little Lena's killer was still very much at large.

Perhaps aware of how lucky he had been to escape the 'nine grams treatment,' Chikatilo did not strike again for three years. In the interim, though, his continued molestation of students lost him his job and it was only the fact he was a good party member that enabled him to get a transfer and work as a travel procurement officer in the huge Rostovnerud factory. The job also gave him the opportunity to travel on company business. The freedom would turn him into a cannibal killer, too.

Chikatilo's second victim was Larisa Tkachenko, a seventeen-year-old girl with a reputation for truancy and offering her sexual favours for food and drink. The thin man spotted her in the city and asked her to come for some refreshments at a café in the nearby woods. Once hidden by the foliage that had previously covered more innocent frolics, he leaped on the young girl and tried unsuccessfully to penetrate her. When she laughed at his failure just as his earlier girl friend had done, Chikatilo's rage knew no bounds. He punched her, thrust dirt into her mouth to muffle her screams and began to strangle her. Suddenly feeling a completely new appetite, he gnawed at her throat, arms and breasts, biting off and swallowing one of her nipples, until she finally died under his frenzied attack...

According to the evidence presented at Chikatilo's trial, the killing of Larisa Tkachenko was the first occasion on which he ate parts of his victims – in particular their sexual organs – while they were still breathing. It would become his technique thereafter to slash his prey with a knife to make them struggle and bleed, thereby providing his climax. A further 'trademark' would be the mutilation of his victim's eyes, as if he feared being watched into eternity.

Any such fears were not, though, evident on 12

June 1982 when twelve-year-old Lyuba Biryuk became Chikatilo's third victim. While on a business trip to the town of Zaplavskaya, he lured the girl into some nearby woods and stabbed her forty times until her convulsions and the streams of blood pouring from the wounds on her chest, stomach and genital area gave him sexual satisfaction. It would be more than a year before her remains were found and, in the interim, Chikatilo had begun to strike with increasingly regularity.

In December of that same year it was the fate of fifteen-year-old Laura Sarkisyan to cross the path of the serial killer who was daily combing the streets of Rostov for prey to lure away to the woods. She, too, was savagely mutilated and her nipples and genitals eaten. Five more victims followed in the summer of 1983, including a sixteen-year-old Armenian girl, a twenty-four-year-old vagrant woman, a nineteen-year-old prostitute and a thirteen-year-old schoolgirl, all found with parts of their bodies bitten off. Chikatilo also killed his first male victim, nine-year-old Oleg Podzhidaev – a fact which apparently convinced some of the police officers investigating the killings of the young girls that he had not been murdered by the same person.

By 1984, Chikatilo's lust had reached fever pitch and the number of his killings accelerated month after month, with at least fifteen between January and September of that year. Females still outnumbered males and the identities of several of these girls – who had their wombs removed – and the boys – with their testicles cut off – all mercilessly butchered to assuage the madman's passions, will probably never be known.

Chikatilo was growing more daring, too, and in April the body of an eleven-year-old girl was found only a short distance from his house, fifty-four stab wounds on her body and his trademark brutalities all over her breasts and vagina. Still the Rostov police, who had been reinforced by Major Mikhail Fetisov from the Moscow Militia, a man who soon became convinced the crimes *must* all have been committed by a lone killer, were no nearer catching the *Lesopolosa*.

In May 1984, Chikatilo took a local mother, Tanya Petrosan, and her eleven-year-old daughter, Sveta, for a picnic in the woods. When the little girl wandered off to play, Tanya apparently lay down and invited Chikatilo to have sex with her. Yet again Andrei failed to get an erection and when the young mother was unable to repress a giggle, he grabbed a kitchen knife from the picnic box and drove it into the side of her head. When, minutes later, Sveta Petrosan returned and saw her mother's defiled corpse lying on the ground, Chikatilo struck again. After beheading the child, he removed the wombs from both bodies and hurried from the wood.

The story of the 'Ripper of Rostov' becomes even more bizarre at this point. While his murder spree was taking place, he was actually arrested and charged with a petty crime. He had stolen a roll of linoleum from work. While the case was pending, seven months passed and Chikatilo was arrested again on 14 December – this time for 'licentious behaviour in public.' He had been spotted by police patrolling the city looking for the mass murderer of girls and seen accosting women at the Rostov bus station. He was sentenced to fifteen days imprisonment.

While Chikatilo was in custody, the hard-pressed police force questioned him about the mass killings and even took a blood sample. Incredibly, it did not match the AB group of the murderer that had been found on the bodies of his victims and was said to be possessed by just six per cent of Russians. Only later would it be realised that the AB sample came from semen and although this was Chikatilo's type, he had a rare blood disorder and the B antigens did not show up in his blood sample.

The sample did, though, seem to match another man in custody who would take the blame that should rightly have been Chikatilo's. His name was Alexei Shaburov, a mentally defective man with a criminal record for stealing cars and inter-fering with small children. Under brutal cross-examination he 'confessed' to having killed several youngsters along with four other men. Once the facts were investigated, however, it was quite evident that neither Shaburov or the others had anything to do with the 'Forest Strip Killer.'

Still undeterred by his run-in with the police – who he clearly now believed were incompetent – Chikatilo returned to the same railway and bus stations he had gone to before looking for victims. His conviction that he was untouchable was underlined again when he was stopped while talking enticingly to a young girl by Inspector Aleksandr Zanosovsky. Asked to produce his papers, Chikatilo revealed documents that said he was a freelance employee of the Department of Internal Affairs, a wing of the KGB. Although they were undoubtedly faked, he was allowed to go.

A month later, Zanosovsky saw Chikatilo in the same locality. This time he observed his man until he had lured a girl to a bar and got her drunk. She had her head in Chikatilo's lap and was allowing him to fondle her breasts when the policeman intervened. As Zanosovsky questioned the suspect, he noticed a briefcase on the seat. In it he found a length of rope, some dirty towels, a jar of Vaseline and a long-bladed kitchen knife.

Even such compromising evidence was not enough to convince the Rostov police they had their multiple killer. And when the briefcase and its contents were inadvertently sent back to Chikatilo's home – where they immediately disappeared – there was nothing left for a prosecution.

The prison sentence and his arrests did, however, have one damaging effect on Andrei Chikatilo – he was fired from his job at the Rostovnerud factory. But his luck had not yet run out and in January 1985 he secured the post of a travelling buyer for the Lenin Locomotive Repair Plant in his old hometown of Novocherkassk. Once again he was free to go where he pleased, his black briefcase and its murderous contents always by his side.

The opportunity for another killing did not present itself to Chikatilo until August 1985. Before heading off on another business trip to the north, he killed an eighteen-year-old girl in Rostov, strangling her and stabbing her thirty-four times. Again he ate her nipples and genitals and ripped out her eyes. Two years later, in May 1987, after apparently having allowed the police manhunt time to slow down, it was the turn of a thirteen-year-old boy to die as a result of his savage lust at Revda in the Ural Mountains.

In 1988 Chikatilo threw any caution to the wind and went on a spree that resulted in eight deaths in places as far apart as Rostov and Tashkent. The following year, nine more bodies were found with his trademark wounds. The police were on the verge of meltdown as the local authorities and relatives who had lost members of their families to the 'super killer' clamoured for action.

Another top man from Moscow was sent to Rostov in the hope that he might stop the ripper's trail of death. His name was Issa Kostoyev, a director of the Central Department for Violent Crime, and his first action was to review every killing that might be attributed to this 'Citizen X.'

He also ordered the local police force out in numbers by day and night. Hidden cameras were set up to photograph likely meeting points. Officers were disguised as decoys and undercover patrols combed the streets. Those working at night were even equipped with night vision goggles.

Despite this flurry of effort, Chikatilo was still able to lure away another unsuspecting victim from the Leskhoz railway station on 3 November 1990. Vadim Tishchenko was a sixteen-year-old schoolboy who had been waiting for a fellow pupil when he made a new 'friend' who slashed his body and bit off his penis before leaving his body in a siding. A week later a similar fate befell twenty-two-year-old Svetlana Korostik who he talked into leaving the station and murdered in the woods.

The killing of pretty young Svetlana was an almost exact replay of Chikatilo's very first murder of the teenager Larisa Tkachenko almost a decade earlier. Now, as then, he cut off the sexual parts of her body and ate them before hiding the body under some bushes and hurrying back to town.

On his way through the fearful streets, Chikatilo was once again stopped by a patrolling plain-clothes officer, Sergeant Igor Rybakov, who had noticed his rather nervous walk. Close up, he could see that the travelling salesman was perspiring and there were spots of blood on his cheek and earlobe. Rybakov checked Chikatilo's papers and despite his suspicions, released him.

No one at that moment, of course, knew of the body lying in the wood.

It was the hawk-eyed director Issa Kostoyev, who had never stopped reading and re-reading all the accounts of the killer's activities, who finally became suspicious after studying Sergeant Rybakov's report of his encounter with the man named Andrei Chikatilo. The coincidence of the death in the woods and then the sight of the blood-splattered man in the vicinity deserved further attention. Of course, he could have cut himself when shaving, but it was a clue, and a welcome one after so many barren months of enquiry.

A list of the murders that could be attributed to 'Citizen X' were then compared to the records of Chikatilo's travels on file at the locomotive plant. The facts were inescapable – he had been in the vicinity of a great many of the murders. The man from Moscow deployed a team of men to follow Chikatilo by day and night.

The day when justice finally caught up with Russia's greatest killer was 20 November 1990 when snow covered the streets of Rostov and the population were still hoping for a good Christmas without the loss of any more of their young men or women. Chikatilo, though, was not in the best of spirits as he was in need of some medical attention and left work early to visit his doctor about a broken finger. The GP could have had no idea as he tended the wound that it had been caused by the last desperate struggles of one of his patient's victims.

Out on the street again – his briefcase under his arm – Chikatilo could not resist the swirl of young people that passed him as he neared the station. Briefly, he chatted to one boy only to suddenly hear a woman's voice calling her son away. He was just about to head off home when three men stepped into his path, flashed their police identification cards, and arrested him. One of Russia's greatest criminal manhunts was about to end.

There were no mistakes this time when Andrei Chikatilo was taken to the Rostov Police Station. The briefcase contained the same contents it had before and this time the prisoner did not even offer an excuse for his behaviour. While Kostoyev began his cross-examination, officers were dispatched to Chikatilo's home and there discovered another twenty-three knives, a hammer and a pair of shoes – all of which were found to match evidence recovered at various of the crime scenes.

According to the subsequent trial, Chikatilo poured out details of his crimes in a scarcely credible confession, listing a total of fifty-three victims, and stating that apart from mutilating the bodies he had eaten the sexual organs of his victims and even had sex with some of the corpses. He indicated to the police where the crimes had occurred, many of them in the local woods. Kostoyev even took his prisoner to several of these sites and had Chikatilo re-enact the killings with models. It was not a pleasant experience for the circle of policemen surrounding the *Lesopolosa* as they watched his frenzied re-enactments.

Even in the face of the mountains of evidence gathered by the police, when the trial opened in April 1992 Chikatilo began denying ever having committed some of the killings. Restrained inside a cage of steel bars in the courtroom – mostly for his own protection from the enraged parents and family members of his victims – he claimed to have had second thoughts about his confession. He was not going to be blamed for every one of the murderers, he said, and began to scream and curse when his claims were dismissed. For much of the hearing, in fact, he would rant and rave and behave outlandishly as police officers and members of the public came and went from the witness box. At one point he interjected:

'I am not a homosexual! I have milk in my breasts. I am going to give birth!'

It is probable that Chikatilo may have been trying to convince the court he was insane. Certainly the evidence suggests his mental condition had deteriorated in the isolation of his cell and the evident hatred directed at him by everyone with whom he came into contact. Marat Khabibulin, the lawyer appointed for his defence, argued that there was no evidence against his client – beyond that of his own words.

Andrei Chikatilo had one last outrage to direct at the public. As the trial neared its conclusion, he suddenly pulled off his trousers and grabbed his penis. Waving it at the public gallery where hundreds of Rostov citizens had sat for the weeks listening to the terrible catalogue of his crimes, he shouted:

'Look at this useless thing! What do you think I could do with that?'

The judge, however, was unmoved by Chikatilo's obscenity. He handed down fifty-two death sentences, adding that he had to drop one of the charges because of 'insufficient evidence.' As he ordered that the prisoner be confined in the Central Prison until the date of his execution, Chikatilo screamed a final accusation that echoed around the room crowded with people still hardly daring to believe their nightmare was at last over:

'Fraud! I'm not going to listen to your lies.'

What personal hell the cannibal killer Andrei Chikatilo lived through during the following months has never been disclosed. Some, though, have suggested that he was completely insane by February 1994 when he was taken into 'Pistol Target Room No. 3,' for his date with the 'nine grams treatment' and his place in history as Russia's greatest serial killer – a statement by then ironically acceptable with the discrediting of the Communist Party and the end of the Soviet Union as a result of Mikhail Gorbachev's twin policies of *glasnost* and *perestroika*.

Satan's Disciples

The advertisement in the August 2000 issue of the fringe heavy metal magazine *Metal-Hammer* was not that different from dozens of others that had appeared in its pages during the rise of interest in witchcraft, black magic and Satanism that had occurred in recent years. Young men and women who were part of an esoteric movement collectively known by the generic name of 'Gothic' or 'New Wave' had, in fact, placed similar ads. The difference was, though, that this message was to bring together a couple who would take murder and blood letting to a new level of depravity. The insert in heavy type read:

PITCH-BLACK VAMPIRE seeks princess of darkness who hates everything and everyone and has bidden farewell to life. Contact Box . . .

The man who had placed the small ad was a twenty-six-year-old German car-parts salesman, Daniel Ruda, and the 'princess of darkness' who came to his bidding was a buxom, twenty-three-year-old dark-haired beauty named Manuela Bartel. A rebellious, strong-willed girl, she had run away from home when a teenager, become a 'Goth' and scoured Europe for new thrills. Two years later the couple would become notorious all over the world as 'Satan's Disciples' following their arrest and trial for the gruesome murder of one of their friends, Frank Hackert . . . and drinking his blood.

It was Manuela who really caught the public imagination and press attention when she first appeared in court in the former coal mining town of Bochum in the Ruhr valley, now a manufacturing centre and home to the giant Opel car plant. With her jet-black hair shaved on one side to reveal an upside down black cross and her deathly-pale face hidden behind dark glasses, she seemed to have stepped straight from the set of a horror movie. Her body swathed in black leather cross straps and occult symbols further enhanced the effect.

Each morning in front of Judge Arno Kersting Tombroke, the girl who wanted to be known as 'Allegra' – after the daughter of the poet Byron – defiantly raised inch-long black finger nails to give the Satanic salute (the index and little fingers pointing upwards) and reiterate her claim to have sold her soul to Satan. Every day, too, little groups of admirers stood silently outside the courtroom or in the crowded public gallery, all dressed in black and clutching roses. The facts of her life that were revealed to the court proved every bit as startling as her appearance.

Manuela had been born, ominously, on 13 November 1978. She was the only daughter of an average working class German family. A small, pretty child who loved animals, by the time Manuela was thirteen she was shocking her parents with her punk haircuts and bizarre clothes and medallions. Although she was selected to attend a gymnasium – the German equivalent of a British grammar school – and appeared to have the ability to go on to university, she dropped out at the age of fourteen. According to some versions of her life at this time she also tried to commit suicide with a drugs overdose.

Despite Manuela's developing beauty and statuesque figure, she appeared to have very little feeling of self-worth, it was later revealed in court by a psychiatrist who gave evidence at her trial. But whatever her insecurities, she decided to leave home at sixteen and ran away to England in 1996.

After a brief stay in London, Manuela got work in Scotland as a chambermaid in a hotel in the Highlands. While in that wild and remote area she had her first brush with the weird. Hearing stories of a curious old man who was tattooed from head to foot, she set off to meet 'The Leopard Man of Skye' as he was known. What she found was a 'strange old bloke' whose stories helped to shape her interest in the bizarre.

When the hotel closed for the winter, Manuela headed south for London again. Here she got work in a Goth club in Islington and became involved in what she later described as the 'underground vampire scene frequented by both vampires and human beings.' She also learned how to suck blood from the neck, as she confessed later.

'I started to meet real-life blood-drinkers and volunteers who offered their veins at "bite parties." We went out at night, to cemeteries, to ruins and in woods. I also slept on graves and even allowed myself to be buried in a grave to test the feeling. We drank blood together from willing donors. Men were always trotting after me – they were my blood donors.'

By the time Manuela returned to Germany she was giving free rein to her fantasies. She sought out other followers of the Goth movement known as *Gruftis* from the German word for 'crypt' and used the internet to contact other 'vampires' who she met in graveyards to 'chat and drink blood.' Taking a step further, she had two of her teeth removed and replaced with pegs onto which she could fix long animal fangs. Her lust for fresh blood grew – although she adhered to what she knew was the cardinal rule of the vampire scene: that 'no one is allowed to drink from arteries.'

In 1999, eager for still more dangerous pleasures, Manuela decided to sign her soul over to Satan. On the night before Halloween she took part in an occult ritual that involved bloodletting. It was at this moment, she explained later in quasi-Biblical language: 'That was when I placed myself in, and swore myself to, the service of our Lord, his will to perform.'

A year later, Manuela met the man who would share all of her fantasies through the small ad in *Metal-Hammer*. Daniel Ruda was a former student turned salesman who had become fascinated by a far right party, the National-Democratic Party of Germany (NPD), which the government was then trying to ban. From their ranks of supporters he had moved on into the skinhead world and then the Goth scene. Quite musically talented, Daniel played for a time in a 'black metal' group called the Bloodsucking Freaks. It was after a review in *Metal-Hammer* that he decided to use the magazine that covered the cult scene to seek a soul mate.

Daniel and Manuela were instantly attracted to one another and were soon having 'super fun' wandering through cemeteries, carrying out midnight rituals and drinking blood. Manuela confided that she had experienced a lust for blood, 'its metallic, salty taste,' ever since she was twelve and had actually begun looking for someone like him when she saw his advertisement.

According to Manuela's testimony in court, the couple decided to get married after she had a vision in which they were commanded to, 'Kill, sacrifice, bring souls.' They chose the sixth day of the sixth month, June, for the wedding and the sixth day of the next month, July, as the day on which they would make a sacrifice to Satan. This gave them the numbers 666 – the Biblical symbol of the Devil. As Manuela explained, 'We had to kill, we could not go to hell unless we did. We intended to commit suicide after the sacrifice.'

From that moment in the summer of 2001 what had started out as an excursion into vampirism became an appointment with violent death and ferocious bloodletting...

The two disciples of Satan did not have to look far for their victim. They chose thirty-three-year-old Frank Hackert, another salesman who worked with Daniel. A quiet, mild-tempered man, his interests were worlds apart from those of Daniel and Manuel. Where they loved heavy metal, he loved the Beatles; and where their taste was for blood and evil, Frank enjoyed television and a few drinks. The couple nicknamed him 'Hacki' and found him an easier target than they had suspected. Manuel said later, 'We thought he was so funny and would be the perfect court jester for Satan.'

The couple carefully planned how to lure Hackert to the small flat in Witten where they had been living since their wedding. Situated between Bochum and Dortmund, the town also had a long history associated with mining now abandoned. It was, though, the downtown area with its reputation for 'real action' and a lively crowd of young people that had attracted Daniel and Manuela and where they made their home.

The Rudas invited Frank to a party on the pretence of sharing a few drinks and listening to some music. Daniel even picked up his colleague from his home and drove him to the apartment. The happy-go-lucky salesman went to his rendezvous with death with a collection of records in one hand and a bottle of red wine in the other. He was never seen alive again.

The gruesome events of that night would not be revealed for some weeks, but at the trial Manuela tried to explain the couple's actions:

'It was not murder. We are not murderers. It was the execution of an order. Satan ordered us to do it. We had to comply. It was not something bad. It simply had to be. We wanted to make sure that the victim suffered well.'

Within hours of killing Frank Hackert, the couple locked up their flat and left Witten in their Opel car heading northeast towards the old border when Germany had been divided in two by the Allies and Russians after the Second World War. They were going on what they saw as a 'pilgrimage' to visit the places in Germany associated with occultism and the far right groups that had once taken up so much of Daniel's time.

The first stop Daniel and Manuela made was at the ancient town of Paderborn with its famous 16th century castle, the Schloss Wewelsbrug. A fortification was said to have stood on the site since the days of the Huns and during the Nazi era, Heinrich Himmler had taken possession of the Schloss and used it as a centre for educating his SS officers into the pagan mysteries that were believed to be the source of National Socialism.

After touring the woody, mysterious landscape with its weirdly shaped rocks that excited the couple's tastes for the bizarre, they drove on past Gotha, the appropriately named town in the Thuringian Forest where the strange *Almanach de Gotha* had been published. They did not stop until they reached the old West German border town of Apolda.

On July 9, just before the couple checked out of their latest motel, Manuela decided to write a letter to her mother. It was not something she had done very often – and would have devastating repercussions for the Rudas as well as the family of Frank Hackert. In the letter, she scribbled a few lines saying that she and Daniel were on a journey of discovery and added, significantly: 'I am not of this world. I must liberate my soul from the mortal flesh.'

The Bartels had, of course, grown used to the eccentricity and wildness of their daughter. But as the couple read the letter over and over again, they both began to suspect that something was wrong, very wrong. It almost seemed as if their daughter wanted to kill herself – as she had tried to do in her teens. They felt they had no alternative but to go to the police with their worries.

The following morning the parents accompanied two officers from the Bochum police force to their daughter's flat in Witten. Sensing no one had been there for several days the policemen broke in unceremoniously. All four people walked straight into a scene from Hell.

The shutters of the flat were drawn and all was darkness inside. Immediately the door was opened and lights turned on horror piled upon horror for the intruders. There was blood splattered on several of the walls. There were streaks of blood in the bathroom and even more in the bathroom. A hideous black and white poster of a hanged woman, which had been hung up over the bath, was also speckled with bloodstains.

In the living room, the scene was even worse. Scattered across the carpet and furnishings were several human skulls, a circle of cemetery lights and long extinguished incense candles. There were also some blood covered vampire teeth and a pair of red contact lenses. Dominating the room was a coffin in which the police investigators would learn later Manuela had often slept during the day to avoid sunlight. Beside it were a number of steel scalpels that glinted dully in pools of blood that were mostly congealed. A bowl that had obviously once held blood lay on its side.

The two policemen almost stumbled over the ultimate horror and at once urged the Bartels to get out of the room. But it was too late – and the foursome in the flat that morning would never forget what they saw next. For just behind the coffin lay a body that had clearly been stabbed and the arms and face savaged with a machete that could be seen on the other side of the room.

Even the two hardened officers were barely able to prevent themselves from vomiting as they counted sixty-six stab wounds on the body. Another scalpel had been plunged into the man's stomach and a pentagram had been cut into the skin of his chest. Beside the corpse lay a handwritten note listing fifteen names. It was not until later that the significance of this piece of paper became apparent . . .

The body, crawling with flies and already beginning to decompose and stink out the room, was that of the gentle, pop-loving Frank Hackert. On the darkened window behind his head were the words, 'When Satan Lives,' obviously written in the dead man's blood.

As soon as the two policemen had got over their feelings of shock and revulsion, they called in to the Bochum Police Station and requested the setting up of a nationwide manhunt for the Rudas. There seemed little doubt they were the perpetrators of the murder and the men took details of the couple from Manuela's parents and removed several photographs of the pair – one taken on their wedding day – from the chamber of horrors that had once been an apartment. They also called the Witten medics to remove the corpse.

The search for the couple did not take long. Daniel and Manuela were hardly inconspicuous with their shaved heads, tattoos, black clothes and silver metal chains. In fact, after leaving Apolda, they had driven less than twenty miles across the old border to the town of Jena on the River Saale, long famous as a focus of liberal ideas in Germany. It was here, on the morning of 12 July, with the car beginning to run low on fuel, that Daniel pulled into a petrol station

The Opel itself was also somewhat out of the ordinary. A Satanic pentagram – like the one carved into Frank Hackert's chest – was stuck in the rear window. Across the car's boot were written the words, 'Grave Beauty.' As Daniel began to fill up the car, the cashier who had looked up to switch on the pump remembered the story on television that morning of a couple of fleeing Satanists who were believed to have slaughtered a man. One phone call and the Jena police soon surrounded and arrested the weird-looking pair as they were poring over a map.

News of the appalling killing and the arrest of the Rudas made front-page news across Germany and throughout much of Europe. When the couple were taken back to Bochum and charged with murder they initially refused to talk – merely making obscene gestures at the police officers and grinning when details of what had been found in their flat were read out from the dossier compiled by the two officers.

The couple were separated and put into different cells. Daniel then became a little more forthcoming about the brutal murder, but showed no signs of remorse. He claimed he and Manuela had to kill Hackert to please Satan. However, while they had been on the run, he had bought a chainsaw, 'because I did not want to be empty handed when the Devil called again.'

Daniel also claimed that he and Manuela had actually attempted suicide several times in grave-yards they had visited as they drove across Germany, 'to be sure to go to Hell.' Manuela agreed with this in a separate statement in which she described how they had both committed their lives to Satanism. While the press clamoured for more details, the trial was set for January 2002.

The media were again out in force when the couple were brought to the courthouse in Bochum, surrounded by hundreds of curiosity seekers and little groups of black-clad Goths who added a sinister touch to the events even before the trial opened. Manuela compounded the drama by demanding that the courtroom windows be blacked out, according to the *Reinische Post* which covered the proceedings, quoting her lawyer: 'She cannot stand the light. She sleeps all day and comes out only at night.' Judge Tombroke dismissed the request but allowed Manuela to wear dark glasses for the duration of the trial.

Throughout, the Rudas never gave up their bold show of defiance, gesticulating, grinning, extending their tongues and rolling their eyes at the journalists. According to them, they were not guilty of murder, on the grounds that they were acting under orders from a higher authority. According to their defence, they deserved lenient sentences on the grounds of mental instability.

Prosecuting counsel, Dieter Justinsky, described how the Rudas had lured their unsuspecting victim to the flat and killed him. He said the method they had used was supposedly based on the album cover *Hammer-Smashed Face* by a band called Cannibal Corpses which featured a heavily mutilated face.

Both defendants had admitted their part in the gruesome killing to the police, Justinsky said. While they had been chatting and listening to music, Daniel had struck Hackert on the head with a hammer. After repeated blows, Manuela said, 'Then my knife started to glow and I heard the command to stab him in the heart. I shouted, "Stab him in the heart," and as Daniel did so, I saw the light in the flat flicker as he was dying. I took this as a sign that his soul was on the way down there.'

It was not long, though, before she felt a sense of disappointment: 'I thought after drinking his blood I would turn into a vampire. As a vampire I would not have needed the streets for my victims.'

Daniel took up the story in his statement read to the court: 'I was in a state of euphoria. After we had

295

stabbed [Hackert] sixty-six times, we collected some of his blood in a bowl and drank it. Then we prayed to Satan. We were empowered by the Devil.'

The former salesman's last words were delivered to a courtroom caught half way between horror and amusement. 'I was merely the tool of the Devil. If I kill a person with my car and half his bloody head is left on my bumpers, it is not the car that goes to jail. It is the driver who is evil. I have nothing to repent because I did nothing.'

Several witnesses were called to give evidence about the couple including twenty-eight-year-old Frank Lewa. He had first met Daniel during his time in the local skinhead / far right scene, but they had fallen out after a row at a party. Lewa told the court about how his former friend had met Manuela through the small ad. In July 2000 he had received a letter from Daniel – just a few days before Ruda and his new bride had killed Frank Hackert.

'In the letter he called me a Judas,' said Lewa. 'He also enclosed a photograph of himself covered in blood and apparently hanging from hooks in the ceiling. He was pointing two gas pistols at the camera.'

In his summing up, prosecutor Dieter Justinsky called the case, 'a picture of cruelty and depravity such as I have never, ever seen. ' Judge Tombroke accepted the couple had committed a 'terrible crime' but believed that the accused were 'humans not monsters and deeply disturbed characters.'

Society had a duty to try to cure them of their severe mental disorders, he said, sentencing Daniel Ruda to fifteen years and Manuela to thirteen years in secure psychiatric units. Neither of them showed the slightest emotion as the sentences were read out.

As the silence in the room gave way to the sound of excited chatter, the couple smiled once more at each other and kissed. They turned and grinned mockingly for a last time at Frank Hackert's parents who had called for them to be jailed for life and sat in a state of bewilderment as the outlandish details of their son's murder had been revealed to them. Then Daniel and Manuela were lead away without another word or gesture as the newspaper and television reporters hurried out of the court to give their story to the world – and add another chapter to the history of blood drinking.

In the aftermath of the case, a number of leading German historians and psychologists examined the facts as part of an ongoing study of Satanism in Germany. It had been estimated that as many as six thousand young people could be involved in the cult, which was said to be most common in the depressed towns and villages of the former Communist half of Germany where unemployment was high and racist elements were more prevalent than in the western sector. The Rudas – this group of experts concluded – might just have been the most visible example of the craze for blood and death.

What has since been pointed out as particularly significant in the case is the list of fifteen names found beside the body of Frank Hackert and the towns that the fleeing couple visited. Both Paderborn and Apolda have been cited as centres where bizarre occult rituals have been reported. Jena – where Daniel and Manuela were caught – has an even more sinister reputation. In 1994, three of the town's youngsters were convicted of the ritual black magic killing of one of their classmates. The trial became known across Germany as 'The Case of Satan's Children.'

Apart from the manner of the killing, there was also another frightening fact that linked the Jena murder to that of the Rudas – the reference to the use of gas pistols firing Zyklon B, the infamous killing agent used by the Nazis in the Auschwitz gas chambers. As the witness Frank Lewa testified, he had received a photograph of Daniel Ruda waving just such pistols.

One question remains – and will probably never be answered, certainly not by Daniel or Manuela Ruda. Was the list of fifteen names those of people due to die next in the couple's bloody pursuit of Satan's approval if fate, and in particular Manuela's letter to her mother, had not intervened?

The Internet Cannibal

There are many bizarre websites to be found on the Internet – a lot of them weird, quite a few outlandish and a number that are undeniably stomach-turning. Probably, though, very few of these sites are more ghoulish than *Flesh and Bone* and *Cannibal Café*, which have become notorious in recent years for attracting advertisements from self-confessed flesh eaters wanting to make contact with people they can eat.

This new twist in the long history of cannibalism became public knowledge in December 2003 when Armin Meiwes, a forty-two-year-old German computer expert, was brought to the Federal Social Court in Kassel, the city reduced to ruins by the Allied bombing raids in 1943 that cost the lives of over ten thousand citizens. Even in a place hardened to death and mutilation, the charges against Meiwes of killing, dismembering and eating another man who had allegedly *agreed* to the arrangement over the Internet, produced a shock wave of horror among the inhabitants.

It was revealed in the *Bundessozialgericht* that Meiwes, an unprepossessing figure who might easily be passed in the street, had posted his 'requirements' in the time-honoured style of a small ad on *Flesh and Bone, Cannibal Café* and one or two of the other similar sites. The message read, 'Seeking young, well-built 18-to-30-year-old for slaughter.' It was claimed to stunned silence in the court that he had made contact with around two hundred would-be 'dinners.'

The facts of the case are certainly stranger than any piece of fiction. Yet, this said, the setting in which the cannibal killer operated might almost have been drawn from the pages of a horror story – in particular Robert Bloch's *Psycho*, filmed by Hitchcock, mentioned in a previous chapter.

Meiwes lived in the little Wurttemberg community of Rottenburg, meaning 'Red Castle,' on the River Neckar. A picturesque medieval town, it boasted the Gothic cathedral of St. Martin, an old castle now being used as a prison, and streets of almost perfectly preserved buildings, which, unlike those in Kessel, had survived the wartime bombings. The manufacturing of machinery, screws, watches and beer has now brought it prosperity.

The town is also somewhat notorious as the home of Hans Georg Hallmayer, known as the 'Witch-Hunter of Rottenburg' who, in the 1570s, had a hundred and eighty alleged witches burned at the stake. Ironically, in 1602, he was accused of witchcraft himself and having sexual relations with the Devil, 'in the assumed form of a hospital maid.' Hallmayer was thrown into prison where he confessed to the pact and died shortly afterwards. His notoriety, though, was almost eclipsed four hundred years later when the facts of the 'Internet Cannibal' became public . . .

The centuries-old house where Armin Meiwes lived was an imposing, half-timbered mansion with a steeply pitched roof, a bank of dormer windows and several tall chimneys. The rows of windows on the isolated building's three floors, all of which were badly in need of repair, seemed to peer like eyes across the surrounding countryside. Indeed, the general air of desolation about the place and its solitary occupant who was rarely seen by local people had earned it the nickname of 'The Ghost House.' This reputation – and the horrors that were later discovered inside the mansion's draughty corridors and warren of forty-four dark rooms – lead to the comparison with the notorious Bates Motel in *Psycho* where the deranged Norman Bates with his mother-fixation, obsession for dressing in her clothes and slaughtering unsuspecting guests, had made his lair. The comparison was, if anything, an understatement.

It was in the privacy of this rotting hideaway that Meiwes made use of the latest technology to contact potential victims to feed his desire for human flesh. Calling himself 'Franky' – after an imaginary friend who had been his only playmate as a child – he used the vast facilities of the Internet to search for like-minded individuals. Although Meiwes later claimed to have made contact with cannibals as far afield as America and Mexico, it was men living closer to home in Europe that really attracted him – especially in Germany, Austria, England and Italy.

Police experts later retrieved details of some of the messages that passed to and from his computer, while other contacts with like-minded individuals he had kept on videotape. Dozens of these were played in court to the judge and packed rows of members of the public, none of whom could quite believe their ears. As if this was not horrifying enough, Meiwes was almost childishly pleased to reveal the contents of other emails during cross-examination. Each and every one of these messages was enough to send a shiver up the spines of the hushed listeners.

One of the earliest responses to his appeal had come from a man who called himself Andreas and said he lived in the busy, modern town of Regensburg in the south of Germany.

'He wanted me to pick him up in a cattle truck and slaughter him like a pig,' Meiwes explained. 'I told him to take the train from Regensburg to Rottenburg. I picked him up at the station and we went back to the butchery at my home. He wanted me to wear rubber boots, which he licked. I wrapped him in clingfilm ready for slaughter. But he backed out at the last moment. So we just fooled around, drank some beer and ate pizza.'

Another German named Dirk, who claimed to be a conference organiser working in Berlin and London, apparently insisted on giving Meiwes specific instructions about *how* he was to be killed before he would agree to be cannibalised.

'Dirk wanted me to pronounce a death sentence on him as they do in court. So I got one made up from a document on the Internet. He came to the house, but then he backed out, too. We ended up going to the cinema to watch *Ocean's Eleven.*'

According to his statement, Armin Meiwes actually found some of the demands of a number of the men who responded to his message too gruesome even for his taste. A man identified only as Alex from Essen asked to be beheaded prior to being eaten. Meiwes gave the excuse he could not do this because his victim was 'too fat.'

Worse still was the scenario proposed by an Italian named Matteo who lived in Rome.

'Matteo wanted me to burn his testicles with a flame thrower. And he wanted me to hammer his body down with nails and pins while he was whipped to death. I found that a bit weird,' Meiwes told his listeners without a hint of a smile on his face.

The cannibal-to-be was apparently being no more humorous when he described how a Russian who offered to provide him with a young boy to be eaten at Christmas had contacted him. However, a few days later, the man told him that the teenager was going to be eaten at a Russian Orthodox feast. Meiwes added, 'I tried the website again after Christmas, but there was no reply. I wondered if perhaps it had happened?'

Some of the emails that the Rottenburg flesh eater sent were equally bizarre and grisly. One, to a man who had contacted him from France, read:

'I hope you come quickly to me as I am a hungry cannibal. Please tell me your height and weight and I will butcher and eat your fine flesh.'

It would seem that that Frenchman did not come quickly – or at all – as Meiwes was soon afterwards tapping out this message to a certain Hansel in Austria:

'Hi! Being roasted alive – that is absolutely a beautiful concept. But keep in mind that with your weight there is about 35kg of your flesh available for eating. If everyone eats 500gms you need 70 people. And there shouldn't be anything left of your delicious flesh. To get such a high number of diners would be difficult. But if you do decide to have yourself slaughtered then please contact me.'

As his electronic correspondence increased, Meiwes was for a time in contact with a man named Stefan who said he lived in Kessel – the very place where the trial was being held. This willing victim, like Andreas before him, had actually visited the 'Ghost House,' gone into the 'slaughter chamber' and been wrapped up in clingfilm. Meiwes said he had even got as far as pinning labels onto different parts of the man's anatomy to indicate the various cuts, when, it seemed, both had a curious change of heart.

'We decided to call it off because it was so damn cold there!' the accused told his astonished audience – some of who were unable to restrain an outburst of amusement mingled with nausea.

All of these incidents were, however, only an aperitif to the main dish – the slaughter of the man whose death put Meiwes in the dock. His name was Bernd Jurgen Brandes, a forty-three-year-old Berlin software designer who died in the old mansion in March 2001. It would, though, be almost two years before the existence of the German 'Internet Cannibal' became known, when he began trawling the net again in the hope of finding another 'meal.'

This time, though, Armin Meiwes' method backfired. Believing he had found a willing victim, he began to describe what he had done with the body of Bernd Brandes. At the other end of the line, a young Austrian student who had answered Meiwes believing the unbelievable was just a joke, realised his contact was deadly serious. Hastily, the young man contacted the police – and in December 2001 one of the strangest of all stories of cannibalism became public knowledge when Meiwes was arrested.

The whole extraordinary story had its beginnings in the strange childhood of Armin Meiwes. Born in 1961, Armin was an only child, doted on by his possessive mother. His father died while he was still young and he had few playmates, as other children were generally wary of him and his remote home. The mansion on the hill had changed little in many years: the paintwork outside and inside was faded and peeling, the lino-covered floors were worn and cracked, and the furniture in every room was ancient and uninviting.

Armin's mother devoted her life to her son and took control of every element of his well being. Local people saw little of the couple and very few people were ever seen going to the house. At the primary school in Rottenburg, Armin was known as shy and withdrawn, but he was also intelligent and quick-witted and had a particular interest in science and mathematics, which he later turned into a mastery of the computer and the Internet. At eighteen, he was called up to do national service in the German Army and proved an exemplary soldier, rising to the rank of sergeant major before completing his term of duty.

Once back home again, though, Armin showed no inclination to break free from the domination of his mother. He showed even less inclination to pursue girls. The piles of mouldering magazines and books found in the cupboards of his bedroom after his arrest indicated that Meiwes had strong homosexual tendencies – though there is no evidence he sought out men while his mother was still alive.

In 1999, Mrs Meiwes died suddenly at the age of seventy-seven. Instead of feeling a sense of relief at being freed from his mother's oppressive presence, Armin was devastated. He inherited his mother's estate – including the gloomy mansion that they had shared – and not surprisingly decided to stay put. Fantasies that he had nursed for years about sexual perversion and flesh eating now began to grow unchecked in his head. He added a number of recent books dealing with cannibalism to the store in his bedroom and trawled the Internet for more information on the subject.

Although his mother was no longer physically in the house, Armin Meiwes continued to behave as if she was. According to information revealed at the trial, he left everything in the house exactly as it had been on the day of her death. The antique furniture began to gather dust where it stood and even the ancient crockery and silver ware they had used for their meals lay on the table where it had been placed on the fateful day. All of the trinkets and old-fashioned objets d'art in Mrs Meiwes' bedroom also remained precisely where she had last put them down.

Only Armin Meiwes changed, from the repressed person he had been to a man now free to live his darkest dreams. In a bizarre recreation of the life of the fictional Norman Bates, the thirty-seven-year-old German began dressing in his mother's clothes, mimicking her walk and imitating her voice in the echoing upper rooms and corridors of the house. As time passed, he turned his mother's room into a shrine and even laid a manikin's head on her pillow as if she was still there. He also began preparing several of the downstairs rooms for a far less harmless and much more terrifying use than they had ever been intended.

The series of emails that would ultimately bring Bernd Brandes to the house of horrors and his date with an appalling destiny began – by a bizarre twist of fate – on Valentine's Day, 14 February 2001, when the Berlin software designer replied to Meiwes' appeal. The early exchanges between the two men appear to have skirted the real issue as they provided each other with details about themselves and their fantasies. Both, though, confessed to being gay and seeking more than just sex in a relationship.

It was not, though, until Meiwes began to describe his interest in food and cooking that voluntary cannibalism – the purpose of the original appeal – entered their dialogue.

'Tonight I am making spaghetti carbonara for dinner,' Meiwes tapped out one day on his computer. A reply appeared on his screen almost at once:

'You won't have to buy meat again if I come to you. There will be plenty left.'

To Meiwes, the words were electrifying. Was his quest at last going to be satisfied? Quickly, he responded with more details about how he would go about the task and what he would do with the body parts. Several journalists in the court noted how Armin Meiwes had smiled broadly and his eyes glinted at the memory as this part of his story was being told.

But there were still other hurdles to be cleared. In one exchange of messages during the summer of 2001, Brandes expressed concern about what would happen to certain parts of his anatomy – one in particular.

'What will you do with my brain?' he enquired.

The recipient had evidently thought about this and the exchange continued as if the two men were discussing the most everyday of subjects:

Meiwes: I'll leave it. I don't want to split open your skull.

Brandes: Better bury it, preferably in a cemetery. Nobody notices skulls there. Or maybe pulverise it?

Meiwes: We have a nice small cemetery here.

Brandes: Or you could use it as an ashtray?

According to the evidence given in the Kessel courtroom, Brandes became increasingly sexually excited as this particular on-line conversation continued. He said he expected to feel a great sense of relief when he was eaten – and added:

'I hope you are serious, because I really want it. My nipples look forward to your stomach.'

Any reservations Armin Meiwes might have had about his potential victim disappeared at this moment, he told the police later. The two men then began to draw up plans for Brandes to travel to Rottenburg the following month. There was no slow-down – or hesitation – in the messages as the month of February gave way to March. One message was almost light-hearted and again produced nervous laughter in the courtroom when it was read out loud:

Brandes: Are you a smoker?

Meiwes: Yes, but my teeth are pretty white.

Brandes: That's good. I smoke, too. I hope you like smoked meat.

Meiwes: Just bring yourself for breakfast.

In the 'Ghost House', Armin Meiwes made his preparations carefully and methodically. In the bedroom where he and Brandes would have sex before the killing ritual, he laid out wires and ropes and set up a small portable electric fire in case the day was cold. He checked the bathroom where he planned to put his victim to bleed to death. He hung a meat hook from the ceiling of what he named the 'slaughter room' – a narrow, third-floor chamber without windows – in which Brandes' corpse would hang before being carved up. Finally, in an ice-cold cellar below the kitchen he built a wooden stand with wire compartments where the man's body parts would be stored until he was ready to eat them.

On 9 March, Armin Meiwes drove to the Rottenburg Station in a fever of expectation. He said his heart did not stop racing until the man whose features he had already seen on his computer screen stepped off the train and introduced himself with a polite shake of the hand. The two men chatted as Meiwes drove through the town and up the hill to his home. Once inside – the court was to hear later – Meiwes, like any good host, gave his visitor a conducted tour of the house. What Brandes thought of the claustrophobic upper chamber, the damp and dingy 'slaughter room' and the mouldering bedroom will never be known.

In his statement, Meiwes said he and Brandes had sex on the bare bed and then went downstairs to the kitchen. There they drank a bottle of schnapps until Brandes agreed he was ready to be eaten. Meiwes urged his victim to take twenty sleeping pills and – in yet another twist to this already grisly plot – to drink a bottle of Vicks Cold Relief.

As Brandes slumped in one of the kitchen chairs, Meiwes said he pulled down the man's trousers. He took a butcher's knife from the table and with one quick slice, cut off his guest's penis. He then bandaged the wound and prepared for his first taste of human flesh. After trying a sliver of the organ raw, Meiwes placed the rest in a frying pan, added some garlic, and cooked it for several minutes. Then, along with the semi-conscious Brandes, he ate the remains.

After the 'meal' was finished, Meiwes said, he

lugged his victim up the stairs to the bathroom, where he filled the bath with warm water. Removing the rest of Brandes' clothes, he put him into the bath to 'bleed out.'

Press reports of the case state that Meiwes left the body in the water for ten hours before he carried out the next stage of his cannibalism. Some of these stories have even claimed that the computer expert whiled away this time by reading a *Star Trek* novel.

By his own admission, Meiwes said he 'finished off' his visitor at 4.15 a.m. He then took the body along the corridors to the 'slaughter room' where he made sure that Brandes was dead by stabbing him in the throat. Then he fixed the corpse to the meat hook and suspended it from the ceiling. For the rest of the night, he meticulously stripped off 65lbs of flesh and placed each cut into plastic bags. These he then placed in his deep freeze in the cellar.

No one, it seemed, had seen the arrival of Bernd Brandes at the 'Ghost House' – and no one enquired when he did not leave in the days and weeks that followed. Indeed, for the next nine months, Armin Meiwes was able to satisfy his desire to eat human flesh virtually every day. Again according to his own testimony, he cooked the body parts in various ways, including roasting, boiling and even grilling one or two bits on a barbecue set up in the garden. He even tried to make flour by grinding up the arm bones of his victim. The remaining items of Brandes' skeleton including the chest and leg bones and teeth he buried in the garden.

When summer turned to winter and Meiwes' appetite for more human flesh took him back on the Internet again, his frankness with the Austrian student soon brought police to his door. The evidence of the emails and videos and a few plastic bags containing the last 15lbs of Brandes' flesh spoke volumes. To the even greater surprise of the officers, Meiwes made no attempt to deny he had killed Brandes – and gave them chapter and verse about the whole gruesome episode.

On 3 December, Armin Meiwes appeared in court at Kessel charged with manslaughter. The case of the 'Internet Cannibal' had been making headline news in Germany and across much of Europe for some time prior to the trial, with arguments raging over whether he could be convicted of any crime. As the evidence seemed to prove that Bernd Brandes had voluntarily and knowingly participated in his own death, it was argued there was no suitable charge under which Meiwes could be convicted.

The unravelling of the details in the *Bundessozialgericht* with the police and prosecution providing a catalogue of Meiwes' actions proved a sensation. The prosecution sought a life sentence, referring to the prisoner as a 'human butcher who had acted simply to satisfy a sexual impulse.' The defence, by contrast, argued that since the victim had volunteered to be killed and eaten, the crime should be classified as a mercy killing, which carried a maximum five-year penalty.

During the proceedings, the object of this intense scrutiny, dressed in a dark suit with a blue shirt and striped tie, sat calm and quiet, occasionally grinning for the photographers allowed into the courtroom before the sessions began and occasionally at officials and members of the public when the hearings started. He first heard the evidence of a doctor who testified that Brandes had died from loss of blood and the medication. The schnapps and the sleeping tablets taken beforehand could not, though, have lessened the pain, the GP added. Three other expert witnesses testified that the accused was fit to stand trial and was not mentally ill.

In the witness box, Armin Meiwes confessed in detail to killing Brandes and told how they had met through the Internet. Brandes had told him that he wanted to be stabbed to death after drinking a bottle of cold medicine to lose consciousness. Meiwes believed that he was not alone in his longing to eat human flesh and claimed that, 'there are about eight hundred cannibals in Germany today.' There were also Satanist groups in the country, he added, that killed small babies, sliced them up and ate them as well as raping women, all part of their initiation rites, 'which have been going on for at least fifteen years.'

Later, during a closed session, the killer sat unmoved when the video he had made of the whole grisly act of butchering Brandes was shown to the judge. It graphically portrayed every act of the terrible drama from the couple making love on the upstairs bed to their last meal together when they had shared the victim's penis. Meiwes' closing statement, however, was made in open session – a mixture of pride and regret and certainly unlike any other heard in a court of law.

'Bernd came to me of his own free will to end his life,' he said without a trace of emotion crossing his face. 'For him it was a nice death. I had my big kick and I didn't need to do it again. I regret it all very much, but I can't undo it.'

On 30 January the debate as to the correct punishment was finally resolved when Meiwes was convicted of manslaughter and sentenced to eight and a half years in prison. The state ruled that he had 'no base motives' in the crime, thus sparing him from a murder conviction.

No sooner had the verdict been announced than the name Armin Meiwes – already nick-named the 'Hannibal of Hesse' by the German press – was being bandied about on the medium that had gained him his place in cannibal history. Dozens of websites sprang up to record the grisly events in Rottenburg and turn their subject into an icon of evil. Within a year, Meiwes had inspired a song, *Mein Teil* (My Portion) by the German band Rammstein, and his life story was being touted as a movie entitled *Your Heart Is Your Brain*, directed by the controversial filmmaker, Rosa von Praunheim, who claimed to have been studying cannibalism for twenty years. Undoubtedly, though, the object of all this intense scrutiny carried one regret with him to his prison cell, as he admitted in his rueful last words in the courtroom:

'If I hadn't been so stupid as to keep looking on the Internet, I would have taken my secret to the grave.'

The Real Hannibal Lecter?

In 2003, the American Film Institute named Dr Hannibal Lecter, brilliant psychiatrist and homicidal genius, portrayed on the screen by the distinguished Welsh actor, Anthony Hopkins, as the 'number one film villain of all time.' No mean achievement for a character who had only arrived in print from the pen of author Thomas Harris in 1981 and was not played on the screen by Hopkins until ten years later. Today, though, Lecter is an icon of villainy, said to have murdered at least twenty-one people and whose very name can make readers and cinemagoers alike shiver in fearful anticipation. Yet at the heart of this terrifying creation lies an enduring mystery – *who* was the original of the most famous cannibal in fiction?

The one person who knows is, of course, Thomas Harris, a quietly spoken and likeable American man of letters who has deflected every question put by the media or members of the general public on the source of his inspiration – in truth, a perfectly understandable reaction. Yet by examining the character and *modus operandi* of Dr Lecter as described in the novels – *Red Dragon* (1981), *The Silence of the Lambs* (1988), *Hannibal* (1999) and *Behind The Mask* (2005) – rather than as he is portrayed by Hopkins (not forgetting Brian Cox in the earlier 1986 movie *Manhunter*, a retitled version of *Red Dragon*), it is possible to build a profile of the world's best known flesh eater. Not to mention looking for clues as to his progenitor among the ranks of the various murderers and serial killers who have practised cannibalism on their victims.

The story of Hannibal Lecter's fictional life is well known to millions of readers. Cultured, brilliant and charming, he is nonetheless a 'pure sociopath'. He eats the liver of a prying census taker with a side order of fava beans and Chianti wine; he murders a police officer and tears off his face to use as a mask; he rips out the tongue of an asylum nurse with his teeth; he replicates the anatomical illustration 'Wound Man' by mutilating a victim; he disembowels an FBI agent with a linoleum knife and later sets a murderous schizophrenic on the agent's family; he induces an annoying cellmate to swallow his own tongue; he persuades a psychiatric patient to eat his own face. In fact, there is almost no human taboo that he does not, with his unique mixture of style and ferocity, tear to shreds.

Thomas Harris has refused all appeals to reveal what, if any, real-life models he had for Dr Lecter. What is known, however, is that he did considerable research at the FBI's Behavioural Science Unit in Washington and studied the case files of a number of serial killers, their habits and murders before writing the novels. Although there can be no absolute certainty, six names stand out above the rest of the murderous group – and it makes interesting reading to examine the credentials of each of them in order to try and postulate a theory to answer this most intriguing of questions.

One man who thinks he may know the answer is the American writer, David Sexton, the author of a thought-provoking book, *The Strange World of Thomas Harris: Inside the Mind of the Creator of Hannibal Lecter* (2003). In this, Sexton claims that Harrison once discussed the origins of his great creation with the librarian of his hometown library in Cleveland, Mississippi, who mentioned a murderer and local legend named William Coyne. Coyne, according to the story, escaped from prison in 1934 and went on a murderous, cannibalistic rampage. Enquiries in Cleveland have failed to produce any more evidence for this claim, however. It seems unlikely, too, that another candidate advanced by Sexton, a Welshman named Jason Ricketts, is any more probable as the progenitor.

Ricketts, from the Grangetown area of Cardiff, was serving a sentence at Cardiff Prison in April 2000 when he attacked and killed thirty-five-year-old Colin Bloomfield from Newport in the vulnerable prisoners' unit. Prison officers had found the victim in his bed with severe abdominal and facial injuries. According to Sexton, Ricketts killed and eviscerated the cellmate, confusing his spleen with his heart.

There are certainly elements in the cases of Coyne and Ricketts that might have been useful to Thomas Harris, but there are stronger cases to be made for four other serial killers – three of them native born Americans – whose foul acts were committed closer to the time when the author was writing his books and were given much greater prominence in the world's media and press. Three have already featured in this book.

The first is the 'Psycho-Killer,' Ed Gein, the Wisconsin farmer whose ghoulish activities were exposed in 1957 and later proved the inspiration for the mother-fixated motel-owner Norman Bates. I believe it is more likely that Thomas Harris used Gein as the model for Jame Gumb, the serial killer that Lecter exposes in *The Silence of the Lambs*. Gein had long thought about a sex change, but instead decided to kill women and dress himself in their skins. He also made a bowl out of a female skull and used the loose ends of flesh to make bracelets and lampshades. Jame Gumb similarly murders women, tears off their skin and weathers the hides – wearing the results in his suburban hellhole until Hannibal Lecter directs Clarice Starling to his door.

Second in the trio of suspects is the Milwaukee killer, Jeffrey Dahmer, 'The Man Who Made Zombies.' Like Ed Gein, Dahmer ate some of the body parts of his male victims and kept strips of their flesh in his refrigerator. He also used various techniques to preserve his 'trophies' – including keeping the men's genitals in formaldehyde – and claimed that eating the flesh of his young victims gave him an erection while 'their spirits kept me vital.'

Again the connection is unlikely. Certainly Dahmer covered his tracks well: dismembering the bodies of his victims, eating the flesh and boiling the skin off their skulls and painting them grey to look like plastic. However, all Dahmer's victims were young men or boys, while Hannibal Lecter tends to target mature men. In any event, the news of Dahmer's crimes did not break until 1992, some ten years after Harris had first created his monster in *Red Dragon*. This said, it is not beyond the realms of possibility that the author utilised some elements in the later novels.

The third man, Andrei Chikatilo, has even become known as 'The Russian Hannibal Lecter' ever since his string of sexually motivated murders came to light in 1992. 'The Ripper of Rostov' killed at least fifty-three young women and children, cannibalising the bodies of many of his victims. In his bloody career from the late seventies to the early nineties, the mild-mannered Russian carried out most of his brutal killings in forestland and used his quiet and obsequious manner to fool both his prey and the police.

It has been suggested that Thomas Harris may well have read about Chikatilo's crimes, as these were widely reported in America at the time of his capture and the revelation of his real name. That said, Hannibal Lecter's method of killing is far more subtle and terrifying than that of the crude and bludgeoning Russian.

The final possibility as the real Dr Lecter is a man whose cannibalism is well-documented, whose methods were ingenious and cleverly carried out and – especially – was a killer who shared Hannibal's taste for freshly prepared and cooked human flesh. Indeed this man, with the curiously apt name of Albert Fish, is even said by some criminologists to have brought similar culinary skills to preparing his cannibal meals as a top chef. The additional facts that Fish was a man of middle age who also wrote about his crimes – copies of these documents are on file at the FBI's Behavioural Science Unit that Thomas Harris consulted – links him still closer to the world's best known fictional flesh eater.

The life story of Albert Fish – for a time before his arrest known in the press as 'The Grey Man' – is certainly as bizarre as any to be found in this book. The fact he committed so many of the warped details of his terrible crimes to paper makes the events seem even more intimate and extraordinary....

The man of whom it would later be said, 'there was no known perversion which he did not practice and practice frequently,' was born in Washington, D.C. on 19 May 1870, the son of a riverboat captain. Albert Fish's childhood was, though, disturbed very early on, as he describes in one of the letters in the FBI file:

'My father dropped dead October 15, 1875, in the old Pennsylvania Station where President Garfield was shot and I was placed in St John's Orphanage in Washington. I was there till I was nearly nine and that's where I got started wrong. We were unmercifully whipped. I saw boys doing many things they should not have done.'

Fish remained at the orphanage on the junction of 20th Street with F Street close to the White House until he was seven. In the intervening years – it was later explained at his trial – the boy got sexual excitement in being abused, which filled his mind with a fascination for sadomasochism. After an increasingly unsettled period as a teenager, he moved to New York at the age of twenty. There he got a job as a painter, married a young girl, Anna, in 1898, fathered six children and for a time appeared to all intents and purposes to be an average US citizen.

Behind the closed doors of the Fish household in Manhattan, however, Albert Fish was growing ever more eccentric and carrying out increasingly perverted activities. Outside, too, it was said he was getting involved in masochistic-homosexual relationships and taking part in a variety of bizarre sexual acts. In 1917, Anna Fish suddenly left home for another man and Albert was faced with the task of caring for six growing youngsters.

By all accounts, Fish did his best for his children, although it seems it was difficult for him to hide his 'strange habits' from small eyes. He began to amass a library of books on masochism, torture and cannibalism and purchased a paddle with a series of iron nails projecting from it. To any casual visitor this might have looked like as an implement to discipline a wayward child – albeit a brutal one. In fact, Albert Fish used it on himself. According to some accounts, he constantly read the Bible and would occasionally cry out, 'I am Christ!' and then force one or other of his children to beat him with the paddle until he bled.

Fish also began to stick needles into his own flesh and a later x-ray examination would show that he ultimately pushed twenty-nine needles so deep into his perineum that they would not come out. The only visible sign of these excruciating fixtures was that Fish 'walked with a strange gait,' a medical report states. Of all these practices he was later to confess in a letter: 'I always seemed to enjoy everything that hurt.'

In his search for more pain, Albert Fish started to answer small advertisements in the New York papers that had been placed by young women looking for lovers and husbands. He wrote back long replies, often full of obscene proposals, with particular emphasis on wishing to be beaten. Several of the women reported him to the police, but aside from a few fines for causing a public nuisance, Fish was put on file as a harmless crank. It would not be until 1938 that he would be revealed as a sadistic serial killer with a taste for human flesh.

The weird career of the Manhattan painter in the intervening years is uncertain because he was constantly on the move across twenty-three states painting houses and using this as a cover to commit more perverted acts and eventually murder. It has been speculated that Fish assaulted as many as four hundred young people, many of them children, and killed at least fifteen girls and boys.

Many of Albert Fish's victims were probably just added to the list of missing persons and never thought about or heard of again. There is, though, more certainty that he was guilty of killing a man in Delaware in 1910, slaughtering a twelve-year-old boy in 1917, and mercilessly torturing and mutilating to death a retarded teenager in 1919.

Details of his atrocities are clearer from 1924. On 14 July, Fish spotted an eight-year-old, Francis McDonnel, playing in the garden of his parents' house on Staten Island. The boy's mother saw a 'gaunt, elderly man with grey hair and a moustache,' in the street and recalled later being 'spooked' by the man's face. It was a face she would never forget.

It was not until later that day, at dinner time, that Mrs McDonnel noticed that her son was missing. By then, her husband, a policeman, had arrived home from duty and he immediately organised a search. Francis McDonnel's body was found in a wood near the family home: it had been brutally mutilated and sexually abused. Although the distraught mother recalled the 'Grey Man,' the police felt he would not have had the strength to carry out such a ferocious killing. Mrs McDonnel believed otherwise – but, in any event, the stranger had disappeared as swiftly and completely as he had appeared.

Three years passed before Albert Fish struck again. This time an even younger child, Billy Gaffney, was snatched from an apartment hallway in New York. When Bill was reported missing, a policeman asked one of his friends if he had any idea where the child was. 'The bogeyman took him,' the infant replied. After closer questioning, a description emerged. The snatcher had been an old man with grey hair and a moustache. The 'Grey Man' was obviously at work again.

The following year, however, Albert Fish committed the mistake that would end his career of bloodshed. His compulsion for writing about his obsessions proved to be his undoing – and one result was probably the most astonishing letter ever composed in the long history of cannibalism.

The series of events began on the morning of 25 May 1928 when a small and quite unremarkable classified advertisement appeared in the Sunday edition of the *New York World*:

YOUNG MAN, 18, wishes position in the country. Contact Edward Budd, 406, West 15th Street.

Hardly unusual among the many other similar appeals in the pages of the tabloid newspaper, it was still destined to start a chain reaction when a smiling, grey-haired man with a drooping moustache knocked at the door of the Budd family's tiny, impoverished home in Brooklyn. The caller introduced himself as Frank Howard and said he was a farmer from Farmingdale on Long Island. He wanted to interview Edward about the possibility of him working in his fields.

Once in the house, however, the man's smiling eyes never strayed far from the Budds' daughter, Grace, a lithe and pretty ten-year-old. Indeed, the caller hardly spent any time at all talking to Edward Budd before offering him a job at fifteen dollars a week, which the young man eagerly accepted.

'Frank Howard' returned to the Budd house again on Saturday 2 June, ostensibly to discuss the job further, although he brought along with him gifts of cheese and fresh strawberries. He encouraged Grace Budd to sit on his lap while she tucked into the tasty fruit.

Just as the kindly farmer was about to leave, he turned to Mrs Budd and asked if Gracie would like to go with him to a party being held by his sister on nearby Columbus Avenue. Encouraged by her husband, who had been completely taken in by the old man, she agreed – and never saw her daughter alive again.

When the little girl and her 'friend' had not returned by the next morning, a police enquiry was instituted. Nothing the man had told the Budds about the party or himself proved to be true – and six years would pass before a word would be heard about either. On 11 November 1934 a letter arrived addressed to Mrs Budd. No mother could ever have received such a weird, obscene and ultimately horrifying communication:

'My Dear Mrs Budd,

'In 1894 a friend of mine shipped as a deck hand on the steamer, *Tacoma*, Captain John Davis. They sailed from San Francisco for Hong Kong, China. On arriving there he and two others went ashore and got drunk. When they returned the boat was gone. At that time there was a famine in China. Meat of any kind was from $1 to 3 Dollars a pound. So great was the suffering among the very poor that all children under 12 were sold for food in order to keep others from starving. A boy or girl under 14 was not safe in the street. You could go in any shop and ask for steak – or chops – or stewing meat. Part of the naked body of a boy or girl would be brought out and just what you wanted cut from it. A boy or girl's behind which is the sweetest part

328

of the body and sold as veal cutlet brought the highest price.

'John stayed there so long he acquired a taste for human flesh. On his return to New York he stole two boys, one 7 and one 11. He took them to his home, stripped them naked and tied them in a closet. Then he burned everything they had on. Several times every day and night he spanked them – tortured them – to make their meat good and tender.

'First he killed the 11 year old boy because he had the fattest ass and of course the most meat on it. Every part of his body was cooked and eaten except the head, bones and guts. He was roasted in the oven – all of his ass – boiled, broiled, fried and stewed. The little boy was next and went the same way. At that time he was living at 409 East 100 Street near the right side. He told me so often how good human flesh was I made up my mind to taste it.

'On Sunday, June 3, 1928 I called on you at 406 West 15th Street. Brought you pot cheese and strawberries. We had lunch. Grace sat in my lap and kissed me. I made up my mind to eat her. On the pretence of taking her to a party, you said she could go. I took her to an empty house in Westchester I had already picked out. When we got there, I told her to remain outside. She picked wild flowers. I went upstairs and stripped all my clothes off. I knew if I did not I would get her blood on them.

'When all was ready I went to the window and called her. Then I hid in a closet until she was in the room. When she saw me all naked she began to cry and tried to run down the stairs. I grabbed her and she said she would tell her mamma.

'First I stripped her naked. How she did kick, bite and scratch. I choked her to death, then cut her in small pieces so I could take my meat to my rooms, cook it and eat it. How sweet and tender her little ass was roasted in the oven. It took me nine days to eat her entire body. I did not fuck her, though I could have had I wished. She died a virgin.'

It took the semi-literate Budd family some minutes to read the letter – and far longer to appreciate its message. Mrs Budd's screams and the howling of her husband, remembering all over again how he had been fooled by the old farmer, soon brought neighbours to their door. The police were hastily summoned and a sergeant read the letter with the same rising anger and bewilderment as the family had done.

Any faint hope the Budd family might have nursed that the dreadful letter was the work of a crank was soon dismissed when it was studied by Detective William F. King of the New York Police Force, who had been following the trail of the 'Grey Man' for some years. The handwriting of the letter also matched that of the killer.

King was even more pleased to see that an

address on the envelope had not been completely erased. Could this be the lead he had been waiting for? Within an hour, the detective was knocking on the door of a boarding house and moments later being let into the room occupied by a certain Albert H. Fish.

When confronted by the burly policeman, Fish grabbed a razor and tried to slash his face. But Detective King had dealt with younger and stronger men many times before during his career in the toughest districts in New York and soon overwhelmed his ageing attacker.

Once in custody, Fish broke down and confessed to being the 'Grey Man.' He also admitted to trapping and eating several other children to satisfy his 'blood thirst.' He described with ghoulish pleasure the joys of eating one little boy's 'pee wee' and a succulent stew he had prepared from the ears, nose, face and belly of another. The roasted *gluteus maximus* was the *pièce de résistance*, he told the astonished Detective King as he took his statement: 'I never ate a roast turkey that tasted half as good as his sweet little behind did.'

When, finally, Albert Fish was asked by King why he committed such horrendous crimes, the old man answered simply, 'You know, I never could account for it.'

As soon as news broke of his capture, the New York papers rushed out special editions, filled with sensational accounts of Fish's exploits. As the day of the trial approached, these stories became ever more bizarre and horrifying. By January 1936 his nick-name of the 'Grey Man' had been transposed across the nation to 'The Brooklyn Vampire.'

One the opening day of the trial, Albert Fish's lawyer James Dempsey lodged a plea of insanity against the charge of murdering Grace Budd. He argued that all his client's years as a painter had caused him to develop lead colic, 'which has turned his brain.' The hushed courtroom then listened to Detective King's statement of the way in which Fish had lured the little girl away from her home and killed her in cold blood and in the most terrible way.

According to subsequent accounts of the trial, it soon became evident to all those who listened to the arguments of both the defence and the prosecution that if Fish had not written the letter to the girl's mother describing the manner of Grace's death he might well have got away with all the other deaths that were now being linked with his name. Dempsey, though, delivered a final extraordinary address to the jury in an attempt to save his client's life:

'In the course of human nature ten of you twelve men will die in full possession of your reason and memory. When that hour comes, when the blood begins to congeal and the breath to fail, when death snaps one by one the strings of life, when you look back to the past and forward to judgement, remember Albert Fish, that when he was helpless and defenceless and pleaded with you for his life, that you said, "Let him live," or "Let him die," and if you said, "Let him die," may He who breathed into your nostrils the breath of life judge you more mercifully than you judged this maniac.'

The lawyer's words notwithstanding, the jury's verdict was predictable. Albert Fish was found sane and sentenced to die in the electric chair in Sing Sing Prison. Curiously, one of the jurors later told reporters outside the court that most of the panel thought that Fish was insane because of the horrors he had perpetrated – though they all believed he should meet his end in the electric chair.

The last hours of Albert Fish were every bit as bizarre as his life had been. Legend has it that the idea of being electrocuted actually appealed to his warped mind and he spent hours discussing with the guards what might happen to his body when the electricity hit it. Would it fry or roast or boil – and how long would he be conscious to savour the experience? It was the ultimate thrill, he said, and the only one he had not tried.

'The Brooklyn Vampire' got his wish on 16 January 1936. But again nothing was straightforward about the event. Tightly bound in the electric chair when the switch was thrown, Fish's body arched forward, but he did not die instantly. The needles sunk deep into his flesh between his testicles and his anus which had never been removed apparently caused a short-circuit in the electricity, charring his whole body. Quickly a second, more massive current was turned on to finish the job.

There are a number of elements in the life of Albert Fish that bear a similarity to that of Hannibal Lecter – his taste for cooked human flesh, his age and the special care and secrecy taken over each killings. It seems more than probable that Thomas Harris would have read the case file on the New York cannibal – but the evidence that he *was* Lecter is difficult to claim without the author's agreement.

What seems more likely to me after examining the details of all the killers mentioned in this chapter is that Hannibal is a composite of them all – and perhaps even a few more – woven together by the author's extraordinary imagination and literary skills to create the pre-eminent fictional villain of the twentieth century. A serial killer and cannibal so unique and compelling that he may well dominate the twenty-first century, too.